Chicago Public Library

Form 178 rev. 11-00

D1088867

THE GREAT
HISPANIC HERITAGE

Pedro Martinez

THE GREAT HISPANIC HERITAGE

THE GREAT
HISPANIC HERITAGE

Pedro Martinez

Tom Lashnits

CHELSEA HOUSE
PUBLISHERS
An imprint of Infobase Publishing

Pedro Martinez

Chelsea House
An imprint of Infobase Publishing
132 West 31st Street
New York NY 10001

Library of Congress Cataloging-in-Publication Data

Pedro Martinez / Tom Lashnits.
      p. cm. —(Great Hispanic heritage)
   Includes bibliographical references and index.
   ISBN 0-7910-8840-5 (hard cover)
   1. Martinez, pedro, 1971—Juvenile literature. 2. Baseball players-Dominican
Republic—Biography—Juvenile literature. I. Series.
   GV865.M355P43 2005
      796.357092—dc22   2005026232

Series design by Terry Mallon
Cover design by Keith Trego

Printed in the United States of America

Bang EJB 10 9 8 7 6 5 4 3 2 1

This book is printed on acid-free paper.

Table of Contents

Welcome to Fenway Park

Hundreds of Boston Red Sox fans, as well as an eager group of sports reporters, stood huddled in their heavy coats at Logan Airport on a cold December evening in 1997. The crowd was waiting for Pedro Martinez, the pitching sensation from the Dominican Republic, who had burned up the mound for the Montreal Expos the previous season. The baseball player had just been traded to the Red Sox by the Expos, and he was coming to Boston to sign his new contract—and pick up a nice big check.

The entire Red Sox Nation—fans from around New England and beyond—hoped that the right arm of Pedro Martinez would help bring victory to their embattled baseball team, especially over the longtime rival New York Yankees. Pedro might even lead the Red Sox into postseason championship play, all the way to victory in the World Series. If he could do that, it would be the first time in 80 years that Boston would bring home the trophy—the first time since

Fenway Park, the oldest stadium in Major League Baseball, is the home of the Boston Red Sox. The first MLB game was played there on April 20, 1912, when the Red Sox defeated the New York Highlanders, 7-6, in 11 innings.

the days when the legendary Babe Ruth played for Boston and the team won the crown in 1918.

The plane from Santo Domingo, capital city of the Dominican Republic, finally landed. A small, wiry man, flanked by Massachusetts state troopers, made his way through the terminal. He greeted enthusiastic admirers who jammed into the airport walkway. "I'm a little tired right now," Pedro Martinez explained to supporters, "but I'm real happy to be in Boston."[1]

The next day, the Red Sox held a news conference at their historic stadium, Fenway Park. The Red Sox general manager, Dan Duquette, officially announced that Pedro would be joining the team. There was a six-year contract that would pay the

26-year-old pitcher a total of $75 million, or an average of $12.5 million a year. The Red Sox then had an option—the choice— to extend the contract for one more year, into the 2004 season, for an additional $17 million. The contract would make Pedro Martinez the highest-paid player in baseball history.

In the Dominican Republic, where the average income is only about $3,000 a year, the news of Pedro's windfall was greeted with jubilation. The night before he flew to Boston, Pedro had celebrated with his brothers Ramon and Jesus, also professional baseball players. The Dominican newspapers hailed him as a national hero and pictured him standing under a waterfall of American dollars. "I'm very happy and enthusiastic," Pedro told supporters in Santo Domingo. "For me it's a triumph for [Dominican] baseball, not only for Pedro Martinez."[2]

Up in Boston, Pedro in turn told the fans: "I always work with a lot of dedication and focus. Now what I want is to reach the World Series with the Boston Red Sox."[3]

Asked how he intended to deal with the pressure coming from those who wondered whether he was worth the record amount of money, Pedro beamed and said, "Play baseball. Once I step inside the white lines I don't think about anything else but beating the other team." And he went on to tell people, "I love the pressure. I like the noise. I think this will be fun."[4]

RECRUITING A STAR

That year, 1997, the Red Sox were in the middle of a big effort to rebuild the team. The previous season, Boston had signed hot rookie shortstop Nomar Garciaparra. Then a new manager, Jimy Williams, came on board. Still, during the 1997 season, the Red Sox had stumbled and faltered. They were soundly eliminated from championship contention in mid-September, when they lost a doubleheader to their archrivals, the New York Yankees.

Boston finished six games below .500 that year, winning less than 50 percent of its games. The Red Sox ended the season in fourth place in the American League East, a discouraging 20 games behind the division winners, the Baltimore Orioles. In the fall of 1997, while other teams battled for the American League Division Series (ALDS), then the Championship Series (ALCS), and finally the World Series, Boston players went home to lick their wounds. And the team's management tried to figure out what went wrong.

A big problem for the Red Sox: They had lost their towering 6-foot-4-inch star pitcher Roger Clemens—known as "The Rocket"—who had left Boston for the Toronto Blue Jays. But now, by signing Pedro Martinez, the Red Sox would boast a legitimate successor to their old pitching ace. Pedro, at 5 feet, 11 inches and 160 pounds, wasn't as big as Roger Clemens. But in every other way he could fill his shoes.

Pedro's specialty was the strikeout—the "K"—and he mixed three devastating pitches to achieve his mastery on the mound. He had a lightning-quick fastball that flashed to the plate at speeds of up to 98 miles an hour. He threw a wicked curveball that started up toward the batter's head, then broke sharply into the strike zone. He also had a deceptive change-up that kept hitters off balance, fooling them into lunging after the tempting but hard-to-hit pitch.

In addition, Pedro Martinez had another weapon, which had nothing to do with his pitching arm, and everything to do with his mental attitude. He was a little guy, almost half a foot shorter than the dominating Roger Clemens—and a lot smaller than most of the other top pitchers in the major leagues. But Pedro would not be intimidated by even the biggest and most powerful hitters. He *owned* the strike zone and didn't let batters inch toward the plate. To keep batters on their heels, he would throw a pitch inside—usually a fastball—and brush the hitter back off the plate. *Take that!* he seemed to be saying, even to the most dominating players in the game.

In recognition of his talent, and his spectacular 1997 performance in Montreal, Pedro had been voted the National

League Cy Young Award winner by the Baseball Writers Association of America, just a month before arriving in Boston. This award goes to the league's most outstanding pitcher of the year. The honor capped off a historic season for Pedro Martinez, the best of his young career.

Pedro had been with the Montreal Expos for a total of four years. In each of those years, he had boasted a winning pitching record, despite the fact that Montreal was a mediocre ball club for most of that time. But during the recently completed 1997 season, while Montreal was limping into fourth place in the National League East division, Pedro was putting up some truly awe-inspiring numbers. He began the year by winning his first eight decisions, the only Expo pitcher ever to start the season winning that many games in a row.

A GAME OF NUMBERS

In baseball, the numbers tell the tale. For hitters, three key figures are batting average, home runs, and runs batted in (RBI). A player with a .300 batting average is a good hitter. He gets 300 hits in a thousand times at bat—or 3 out of 10. When Boston Red Sox outfielder Manny Ramirez won the batting title in 2002 with a .349 average, he was getting hits more than a third of the time.

Home runs show power. Babe Ruth's 1927 season record of 60 home runs stood until 1961, when Roger Maris hit 61. Mark McGwire and Dominican-born Sammy Sosa galvanized fans when they chased each other in surpassing the record in 1998: Sammy Sosa ended up with 66, while Mark McGwire topped out at 70. In 2001, Barry Bonds, the San Francisco slugger, eclipsed them both with his record of 73 home runs.

It stands to reason that good hitters knock in a lot of runs. Manny Ramirez, Mark McGwire, and Sammy Sosa have all been RBI leaders in their respective leagues.

Pitchers rely on different numbers. The won-lost record is

Commenting on how Martinez bullied and baffled hitters, New York Mets outfielder Lance Johnson said after his team lost to Pedro in April: "He wore us out. He throws everything, and he throws it all for strikes. He put it where he wanted to. You have to hope he makes a mistake, and he didn't make any with me."[5]

Perfect Pedro was finally beaten by the New York Mets a month later, on May 28, but his domination on the mound continued throughout 1997. Martinez pitched for the National League in the All-Star Game, facing three batters. He struck out Alex "A-Rod" Rodriguez; got slugger Ken Griffey to fly out; and then struck out big-muscled home run king Mark McGwire.

That's when people started speculating that Pedro Martinez would likely win the Cy Young Award. One of the

crucial, because baseball is a team sport, and above all else the pitcher's job is to win the game. But this is also an imperfect measure of performance, because so many factors come into play during a game. Who's the better pitcher? The one who is tagged for seven runs but wins 9-7, or the one who only lets in a single run but loses 1-0?

Other numbers measure pitchers more directly. The fewer walks a pitcher gives up, the better control he has. The number of strikeouts he throws shows how dominant he is. A hurler who strikes out an average of one batter per inning, or nine strikeouts in a game, is doing a fine job.

The purest measure of performance is earned run average (ERA). Earned runs are runs that hitters "earn" off a pitcher with hits and walks, as opposed to "unearned" runs that score on errors. A pitcher's ERA tells how many earned runs he allows during a nine-inning game. When Pedro Martinez posted an ERA of 1.90 in 1997, it meant he allowed his opponents an average of only 1.9 runs per game. That's an impressive number—good enough to win the Cy Young Award!

most important measuring sticks for a pitcher is his earned run average (ERA), which tells how many runs a pitcher allows in a game (see "A Game of Numbers" sidebar on pages 10–11). At the All-Star break, Pedro had the best ERA in the majors. He also led the league in shutouts, and he was well on his way to becoming the strikeout ace of the major leagues.

Everyone was beginning to realize that Martinez ranked among the most impressive pitchers in baseball. As Felipe Alou, manager of the Montreal Expos, pointed out, "Something to remember is that when you talk about dominant pitchers today—Greg Maddux, Randy Johnson, Roger Clemens—you're talking about veterans. The thing about Pedro is that he has just reached that plateau and he's 26 . . . He's learning. He's getting better. And he's dominant now."[6]

Pedro improved his chances for the Cy Young Award on September 25, 1997, when he struck out nine Florida Marlins in a home game in Montreal, to surpass 300 Ks for the season—only the fourteenth pitcher in major league history to reach that milestone.

Pedro finished the 1997 season with a total of 305 strikeouts—a Montreal team record—and he led the majors with a 1.90 ERA. Martinez was the first pitcher in 25 years (the last was Philadelphia Phillies pitcher Steve Carlton in 1972) to produce an ERA of under 2.00 and also chalk up more than 300 strikeouts.

In November 1997, when votes came in for the National League Cy Young Award, Martinez took 25 of the 28 first-place votes, and 134 total points in the balloting. Veteran pitcher Greg Maddux of the Atlanta Braves—who had won the award four years in a row from 1992 through 1995—came in second with 75 points.

Pedro Martinez thus became the first and only Montreal Expo—as well as the first and only pitcher from the Dominican Republic—to win a Cy Young Award.

As the dominating Dominican reaped the rewards of his pitching performance, he also thought about his future. He had earned $3.5 million in 1997 with the Montreal Expos—the highest paid player on the team. But he knew that with his arm, he could make a lot more. He also realized that the Montreal Expos, located in a city where ice hockey (not baseball) is king, would never command the support of a large and loyal fan base and never attract enough top players to get to the World Series. The Expos had lost some $13 million that year. Executives were looking to *cut* the payroll, not add to it.

If Pedro ever wanted to pitch in the postseason, and make the money he deserved, he would have to go somewhere else. His contract with the Expos was coming to an end. And so he started looking around for another place to play.

The list of suitors was long. The San Diego Padres—who that year had had the worst pitching season in their history with a team ERA of 4.98—expressed an interest in the man from Montreal. The Cleveland Indians, who had won the American League Championship Series (the ALCS) but lost in the World Series, were prepared to make a bid. The Texas Rangers, the New York Mets, the Baltimore Orioles, all expressed interest in the 26-year-old. Even a tight-lipped representative from the mighty New York Yankees said, "He's a player that's a bona fide starter. We would have to have an interest. That's all I'm going to say."[7]

Officials from the Los Angeles Dodgers also admitted they were thinking about Pedro Martinez. Pedro had started his career with the Dodgers, and his older brother Ramon was still a pitcher on the team. Pedro made no secret of his desire to be reunited with his brother, so everyone knew he would be happy to go back to California.

But Boston Red Sox General Manager Dan Duquette also had Pedro in his sights. And Pedro knew all about Duquette, because Duquette had been general manager of the Montreal Expos four years earlier, in 1993, when Montreal traded second baseman Delino DeShields to the Dodgers for Pedro. And so Dan Duquette's personal touch—along with a baseball stadium full of money—brought Pedro Martinez to Boston that

In December 1997, the Boston Red Sox traded for pitcher Pedro Martinez and signed him to a record six-year, $75 million contract. Martinez is pictured here during his American League debut in a spring training game against Minnesota.

cold December evening, ready to lead a new-and-improved Red Sox team to greater glory.

As Pedro left Boston to go home, just a few days after he arrived, Red Sox fans once again mobbed him at the airport.

"They were grabbing me, asking for my autograph," recalled Martinez. "Asking questions about the team, asking if I was going to be their savior, the next Roger Clemens.

I said, 'No way, I can't be Roger Clemens. I can only be Pedro Martinez.'"[8]

FIRST SEASON IN BOSTON

Pedro spent the winter in Santo Domingo working out with his older brother Ramon, who was a star in his own right for the Dodgers. Pedro lived in a duplex apartment in one of the wealthier sections of the Dominican Republic's capital city. Six days a week, Pedro and Ramon would drive over to the Olympic training center in Santo Domingo. Their coach would put them through a tough two-hour workout. The two of them would run four or five miles, then they'd stretch and go through an exercise regimen designed to increase their strength and agility.

After sweating through the morning at the Olympic center, the two brothers would drive home, eat lunch, and go back to work out at Ramon's gym. "Six days a week we work, one day we relax," Pedro told a Boston sportswriter. "Stop working and you go right back where you came from—nothing."[9]

Pedro did take time out to play in the Dominican League, where a number of Hispanic major leaguers play in the off-season, helping their local teams be more competitive in the playoffs. Pedro pitched for the Licey Tigres in Santo Domingo, where for just a few pesos fans could get in to see their new million-dollar hero.

Meanwhile, the press began talking about how the Red Sox now, finally, had to be taken seriously as a contender. The 1998 season would feature Cy Young Award winner Pedro Martinez, first and foremost. He was backed by starting pitchers Tom Gordon and Tim Wakefield, as well as veteran hurler Bret Saberhagen, who had won the Cy Young Award in 1985 and 1989. Then there was shortstop Nomar Garciaparra, veteran slugger Mo Vaughn, and solid third baseman John Valentin.

So as the new Red Sox season began in the spring of 1998—80 years after their last World Series victory—there was hope in the air. The Red Sox had a real baseball team again.

Manager Jimy Williams tapped Pedro to pitch on opening day, an away game in Oakland, California, and Boston's new pitcher did not disappoint. It was the fourth inning before the Oakland Athletics even got a hit—a weak single looped into left field. And Oakland could not score a single run against Pedro, as the Dominican struck out 11 batters in seven innings and won the game for the Red Sox in a shutout, 2-0.

Said the impressed Oakland rookie A.J. Hinch: "Nobody would want to make a living facing *that* every night. I don't care, rookie or veteran, he was tough on all of us. He showed why he's paid the way he is. He deserves the accolades."[10]

Unfortunately, the Red Sox lost six of their next eight games on the road, including a pitching duel between Pedro Martinez and Chuck Finley of the Anaheim Angels. Pedro struck out nine batters that day and gave up only one run in seven innings. But the Red Sox hitters failed to give Pedro any run support, sending only one man across home plate. After Pedro left the game, the contest went into extra innings, tied at 1-1, and in the bottom of the tenth, an Anaheim single brought in a run. The Angels won the game, 2-1.

A few days later, on April 10, the Red Sox came back to Boston and won their home opener against the Seattle Mariners, in a game featuring a ninth-inning grand slam home run by Boston slugger Mo Vaughn. The next day brought Pedro to the mound, the first time he pitched in a Red Sox uniform in Fenway Park. When Pedro walked out on the field to start the first inning, an enthusiastic crowd stood up and cheered and roared a real Red Sox welcome. Fans from Boston's Hispanic community waved Dominican flags in the stands.

At the end of the third inning, after Pedro had struck out three Mariners in a row, the fans gave him another standing ovation. He enjoyed *another* standing ovation in the eighth inning, when he posted the 1,000th strikeout of his career, and *another* when he came out to pitch in the ninth inning, and yet *another* when he got slugger Ken Griffey to foul out to end the game. Pedro logged 12 strikeouts that day, winning the game, 5-0, for the Red Sox with a two-hitter.

Now, Pedro had truly arrived.

These two Red Sox victories began a promising stretch—Boston won 20 of its next 26 games. But as good as the Red Sox were, the Yankees were better. The team from the Big Apple took over first place in May, and before June was over, the Yankees led the Red Sox by nine games in the American League East division.

Nevertheless, Pedro proved his worth. He suffered from a stomach problem and a shoulder problem during the season, but neither one slowed him down much. Throughout the summer of 1998, the headlines read:

Martinez Comes Up Aces
Martinez Wins Pitching Duel
Pedro Punishes Montreal
Martinez Dunks Anaheim
Martinez Continues Hot Streak

The Yankees would win the American League East. But all was not lost for the Red Sox. Since both baseball leagues—the American and the National—have three divisions (East, Central, and West), a wild-card team is selected to fill out the fourth position in the division playoffs. The wild card is the second-place team with the best record. In 1998, Boston won the spot, as, fittingly, Pedro won his nineteenth game of the season against the Baltimore Orioles to clinch a berth in post-season play for the Red Sox.

So that fall, instead of heading home in defeat as they had the year before, the Red Sox would challenge the Cleveland Indians, winners of the American League Central.

The American League Division Series (ALDS) is a best-out-of-five contest. During the regular season, Boston boasted an 8-3 record against the Indians. Surely, if the Red Sox had won 8 out of 11, they could win 3 out of 5. Plus, the Red Sox had an ace in the hole. As expected, manager Jimy Williams tabbed Martinez to start the first game in Cleveland.

After six years in the major leagues, Pedro would finally get his chance to pitch in the playoffs.

In that opening game, Pedro threw five scoreless innings, while Boston hitters drove in eight runs. Martinez then let in a couple of runs, but Boston went on to win the game easily. "His

PEDRO MARTINEZ'S LEGACY

FORMING A BOND WITH THE FANS OF BOSTON

Pedro Martinez, who has never been married, stays close to his family. Every year he spends the off-season in the Dominican Republic. He kept a home in Boston, where he lived with various family members, including at one time his brother, Ramon, and also his sister, Anadelia. Pedro also had cousins living in Providence, who came to visit, and a cadre of close friends. Although the pitcher was occasionally seen in Boston driving his black Mercedes, he was never one for going out much. "I'm not a club type of guy,"* Pedro has said.

Pedro did, however, form ties with Boston's Dominican community. He spoke to children at local schools and visited patients at area hospitals. He established a charitable foundation in Boston, focusing on the needs of the Latin community. He also built a church in his hometown of Manoguayabo, donated computers to schools, and sponsored a sports center. When Hurricane Georges swept through the Dominican Republic in 1998, Pedro gave $100,000 to the relief fund.

Pedro has said he likes the city of Boston—except for the climate. He hates the cold weather and could often be seen bundled up in the Boston dugout. But "the summer, the trees, the river . . . it's a beautiful city, it's clean."**

concentration was there," said Indians shortstop Omar Vizquel about Pedro. "He was locked in, making good pitches all over. Sometimes you think you'll get him, but he makes that perfect pitch all the time."[11]

In Game 2 of the series, the Red Sox jumped ahead to a 2-0 lead in the first inning. Now things were looking *really* good. But Red Sox pitcher Tim Wakefield didn't last long, and the Boston bullpen failed to stop the Cleveland batters. The Red Sox lost, 9-5.

Pedro also formed a special connection with the fans. "I like the fans here," he said. "I have a passion for the game. I play for myself, my team-mates, and my family, but I also feel a responsibility to my team and the fans."***

Before Pedro showed up in Boston, the Red Sox had very little connection with New England's sizable minority community—not just in Boston, but in Providence, New Bedford, Worcester, and Hartford. But from the moment Pedro made his debut at Fenway Park, in April 1998, Dominican flags showed up in the stadium. Chants of "Pe-dro! Pe-dro!" were heard loud and clear in the stands. And fans mounted the "K" placards to mark Pedro's strikeouts.

As a restaurant owner in the largely Latino Jamaica Plain section of Boston told one sportswriter in 2004: "No one in this community cared about the Red Sox before. Pedro revived the Hispanic community in the city. Everyone in the community started watching the Red Sox and going to the games."†

  * Dan Shaughnessy, "A Conversation with Pedro Martinez—The Man at Ease," *Boston Globe*, October 3, 1999.

  ** Ibid.

  *** "Festivities at Fenway Take on a New Flavor," *Boston Globe*, April 12, 1998.

  † "Newsmakers: Pedro Changed Face of Red Sox," *Houston Chronicle*, November 8, 2004.

In 1998, the Boston Red Sox earned a playoff berth for the first time in three years. Despite facing the Cleveland Indians—a team they posted an 8-3 record against during the regular season—the Red Sox lost the American League Division series, three games to one. Pictured here is Cleveland right fielder Manny Ramirez, who hit two home runs in the Indians' 4-3 win in Game 3 of the series.

With the series tied at 1-1, the contest moved to Boston for Game 3, where the Red Sox would have home-field advantage. But despite a ninth-inning home run by Nomar Garciaparra, the Red Sox lost, 4-3.

Boston was down in the series 2-1. And now things were looking bad. One more loss and the Red Sox were finished.

Starting pitchers typically get four days rest between their outings, and so Pedro was originally scheduled to pitch Game 5 of the series. But there might not *be* a Game 5.

Facing elimination, Boston fans cried out to manager Jimy Williams to go with Pedro Martinez—even though their hero would only have three days rest. Martinez himself volunteered for the job, saying he was ready to play.

Williams resisted the pressure. He kept Pedro on the bench and started another hurler. Sure enough, Boston lost to the Indians, 2-1, as Cleveland's pitching ace Bartolo Colon (who, like Pedro, hails from the Dominican Republic) kept Boston bats in check, with only a Nomar Garciaparra home run putting the Red Sox on the board.

The 1998 season was over. The Cleveland Indians, who beat the Red Sox, went on to lose the ALCS to the powerhouse Yankees, who would in turn capture the World Series.

Of course the Red Sox were disappointed. But they had a lot to be proud of, too. The previous year, they had finished in fourth place in the American League East. This year, they came in second and made the playoffs. They were now being taken seriously as a contending team—thanks in large part to Pedro Martinez, who brought his passion for winning to this long-suffering ball club.

Pedro ended the season with a won-lost record of 19-7. He posted an ERA of 2.89—an impressive average but not quite as good as his ERA of 1.90 in 1997. He also managed 251 strike-outs—a lot for a good pitcher but less than his 305 in 1997.

Pedro was still a top prospect for the Cy Young Award. But when the votes came in, it was former Red Sox pitching ace Roger Clemens, now with the Toronto Blue Jays, who won the prize. Pedro took second place. And so with this "almost" 1998 season under his belt, Pedro jetted back to the Dominican Republic—the place where he was born, where he grew up, and where he learned how to play baseball.

Where Baseball Rules

Pedro Martinez was traded to the Boston Red Sox after playing four years in Montreal. But to see where Pedro really comes from, you don't go to Canada; you instead head south—past the Bahamas to the West Indies and the island of Hispaniola.

About the size of South Carolina, Hispaniola sits between Cuba and Puerto Rico in the Caribbean Sea. The island, which consists of fertile valleys separated by rugged mountains, was discovered by Christopher Columbus on his first trip to America in 1492. Today, it is divided into two countries: Haiti on the western side, and the larger Dominican Republic to the east.

Pedro was born Pedro Jaime Martinez, on October 25, 1971, in Manoguayabo, a small village on the outskirts of Santo Domingo, capital city of the Dominican Republic. This capital was founded in 1496 by Bartholomew Columbus, Christopher's brother, and despite periods of violence, epidemic, dictatorship, and revolution

In the Dominican Republic, children begin playing baseball at an early age. The island nation has sent hundreds of baseball players to the major leagues, including Pedro Martinez. Pictured here are two children playing baseball at the Complejo Deportivo baseball camp in San Pedro de Macoris, Dominican Republic.

over the centuries, it has been occupied ever since—the oldest continuously inhabited city in the Americas.

Today, the Dominican Republic is a democracy—its constitution dates to 1966—and its 8 million inhabitants, although largely of mixed race, are almost uniformly Spanish-speaking Roman Catholics. The country enjoys a tropical maritime climate, and in the winter plays host to its share of American tourists; but it also lies in the middle of the Caribbean hurricane belt and is subject to severe storms in late summer and fall.

This lush but sometimes storm-battered country is poor, with at least a quarter of its inhabitants living below the poverty line. Residents rely on tourism for their income, as

(*continued on page 26*)

A CIRCLE OF FRIENDS

THE ALOU BROTHERS PAVE
THE WAY FOR PEDRO

The three Alou brothers—Felipe, Matty, and Jesus—were heroes to Pedro as he was growing up in the Dominican Republic. Later, eldest brother Felipe Alou was to become Pedro's manager, while Felipe's son, Moises, played as Pedro's teammate.

Felipe, Matty, and Jesus Alou are not only pioneers—among the first Dominicans to make it to the major leagues—but in 1963, when youngest brother Jesus was called up to San Francisco, the three of them briefly formed the only all-brother outfield ever to play in the majors.

Felipe, the oldest, was a six-foot-tall slugger. As a youngster in the Dominican Republic, he dreamed of becoming a doctor. But he showed a talent for baseball, and when his team won the gold medal in the Pan American games, his course was set.

Felipe made his major league debut in 1958—the year the Giants moved from New York to San Francisco. In 1962, he played in the All-Star game and went to the World Series. Felipe Alou's finest year was 1966—after he was traded to the Braves—when he batted .327 and again was named an All-Star.

Middle brother Matty, three years younger than Felipe, was the smallest and fastest of the three—only 5 feet, 9 inches and 160 pounds. He was called up to the Giants in 1960 and played alongside Felipe in the outfield. Matty and Felipe played together for the next four seasons—including the 1962 World Series.

Matty didn't really come into his own, however, until after he went to the Pittsburgh Pirates. In 1966, he led the National League in batting with a .342 average (beating out his brother) and for several years after that Matty remained one of the top hitters in the league. He made the All-Star team in 1968 and 1969, and in 1972, in the twilight of his career, he went to the Oakland Athletics, where he helped the team win its first World Series.

Jesus Alou, the youngest brother, went to the Giants in 1963, and briefly found himself in the outfield with his two brothers. When eldest brother Felipe was traded to the Braves, Jesus replaced him as the Giants' right fielder. Jesus played for the San Francisco Giants for six years, then moved to the Houston Astros.

After their playing careers were over, two of the Alou brothers went on to manage baseball teams. Matty returned to the Dominican Republic, where he coached a team in the winter leagues. Felipe migrated to Montreal and went to work in the team's minor league system. In 1992, Felipe took over as manager of the Expos, and he soon became known for spotting and developing new talent, including pitcher Pedro Martinez, as well as his own son Moises, who had been drafted by the Pittsburgh Pirates and then traded to the Expos.

Under his father's tutelage, Moises became a top hitter and was named an All-Star in 1994. For the 1997 season, though, the year before Pedro arrived in Boston, Moises Alou moved to the Florida Marlins, where he played in the World Series and hit three home runs to help the Marlins win the championship. Moises was later traded to the Houston Astros and then the Chicago Cubs, where he played with a fellow Dominican, home run hitter Sammy Sosa, and was again an All-Star.

Meanwhile, Felipe was selected manager of the year in 1994 for his efforts in Montreal. He continued to make the best of a team that was constantly starved for cash to pay top talent—including Pedro Martinez, who left for big bucks in Boston, as well as his own son Moises, who had parted for more money in Miami.

In 2001, Felipe Alou was replaced as Expos manager. The aging baseball legend decided to retire. However, less than two years later, he was lured back to San Francisco to manage the team where he had started his career more than 40 years before. In 2003, his first year as manager, Alou led the Giants into the playoffs, where they lost to the World Series-winning Florida Marlins.

In 2005, Moises Alou signed a contract with the San Francisco Giants. Father and son were reunited. The two men, plying familiar fields, have said they plan to finish their careers together—a family to the end.

(*continued from page 23*)
well as exports of agricultural goods, such as sugar, coffee, and tobacco.

In the 1970s, when Pedro was a little boy, the Martinez clan formed a typical Dominican household. Pedro's parents, Paulino and Leopoldina Martinez, owned a modest farm in Manoguayabo. Pedro's father, Paulino, brought home a small paycheck from his job as a janitor in the local school, while the family scratched out their food from two acres of fields.

Pedro had two older sisters and two older brothers. Ramon was the eldest brother. Nelson was a year younger than Ramon. Later, when Pedro's little brother, Jesus, came along, there were eight people living in the small Martinez house. They had no indoor plumbing, no indoor toilet.

Facing a future with limited possibilities on their own island, many young Dominicans wanted to leave their country to find opportunity elsewhere. The ultimate dream was always to immigrate to the United States. That's where people could get a decent job and build a better life for themselves. And that's why the Dominican Republic has come to boast another important export besides sugar and coffee: baseball players. In the eyes of many Dominican kids, the best way to get to America—the *only* way to get to America—is to play baseball, and become good enough to be picked up by a major league team and brought north to experience the riches of the mainland.

Back in the 1950s, before the Dominican Republic was discovered by major league scouts, Pedro's father, Paulino, had played baseball. He'd been a pitcher for several local teams and played in the same leagues with several Dominicans who later made the leap into professional ball, including three famous Alou brothers—Felipe, Matty, and Jesus—as well as the great San Francisco Giants pitcher Juan Marichal.

A number of people thought Paulino, too, was good enough to play baseball in the United States. Felipe Alou, eldest of the Alou brothers and a major league All-Star in the 1960s—and later manager of the Montreal Expos when Pedro was on the team—maintained that Paulino was plenty talented enough to pitch in the major leagues. Paulino was once even asked to show off his pitching talent to the scouts. "But I was too poor to leave the country," Pedro's father recalled. "When the Giants invited me for a tryout, I didn't have cleats. So I couldn't go."[12]

Older son Ramon once said, "A lot of people told me how good he was." And Ramon credited his father for inspiring his own jump to the majors. "That made me want to play, and be somebody famous."[13]

Paulino taught all of his boys how to play baseball. He encouraged them to work hard, practice a lot—and above all, have fun. But as much as Paulino coached and inspired his sons, he could not afford to buy them much baseball equipment.

Without proper bats and balls, the Martinez brothers practiced by throwing and hitting almost anything that was round. They used rocks, rolled-up socks, pieces of fruit, rubber balls, even the heads they tore off their sisters' dolls. They used an old broom handle for a bat. "We played baseball all the time, in the streets or wherever," older brother Ramon remembered. "I grew up this way. I was always active, playing with my friends, playing in the parks that weren't in very good condition."[14]

Pedro later acknowledged: "When my sisters came home from school, they'd find [dolls] with no head and they would go, 'Mommy, Mommy!' I would take anything that was round to play baseball. That's the passion I had."[15]

Despite their poverty, the Martinez offspring enjoyed a happy childhood. When Pedro was nine, however, his parents got divorced. Pedro relied on his older brother Ramon for guidance and security, to help him through his childhood—and to continue to teach him to play baseball. "Our parents cared for us and did a great job instilling values in us," Pedro once told the *Boston Globe*. "But Ramon is the biggest reason I have gotten where I am. He is the great one in this family."[16]

RAMON LEADS THE WAY

All three of Pedro's brothers—Ramon, Nelson, and Jesus—were tall and strong, and they all played baseball in the Dominican Republic. Ramon, the oldest, was the star. He was tall, at six foot four, and slim, and wanted to be a pitcher like his dad. He could throw hard, and he blistered his fastball right past most of the Dominican hitters. By age 15, Ramon was earning money pitching for various teams around Santo Domingo.

By the early 1980s, when Ramon started playing seriously, baseball had become such a popular pastime in the Dominican Republic that scouts from the United States were prowling the island on the lookout for good players. If Juan Marichal and Felipe Alou had come from the Dominican Republic, they reasoned, then there must be plenty of other good players there as well.

Soon the American scouts began to eye Ramon Martinez. One in particular, Ralph Avila of the Los Angeles Dodgers, was impressed with how the tall, skinny pitcher kept striking out batters. In 1983, Avila invited Ramon to a camp sponsored by the Dodgers. At the baseball academy, Ramon would get instruction on the finer points of the game.

The young prospect already knew how to throw hard, and he had been taught the basics by his father. But now he really learned how to pitch with intelligence and finesse. Coaches told him that location is everything. It's not how hard you throw, so much as *where* you throw it. You pitch to where the batter has the least balance.

After his session at the academy, Ramon played for an adult team, the Manoguayabo Braves, and he soon became the best pitcher on the squad. Younger brother Pedro would often come around to watch Ramon play, and he would throw the ball around himself. Meanwhile, Ralph Avila was chosen to manage the Dominican Republic's national team that would play in the 1984 Olympics in Los Angeles. Avila picked Ramon to be one of the pitchers on the Dominican team.

Accepting the challenge, 16-year-old Ramon Martinez

traveled to Los Angeles, stepped onto the mound as a boisterous crowd cheered him on, and promptly pitched three scoreless innings against the team from Taiwan. His Olympic performance impressed the Dodgers, and they soon offered Ramon a minor league contract.

Professional baseball players typically work their way through four levels of baseball before they get to the big leagues: rookie ball, Class A, Class AA, and Class AAA. As players progress through each league, the level of play gets better and the competition gets fiercer. Ramon spent his rookie year of 1985 at home with the Santo Domingo Dodgers.

Again, Pedro followed his older brother to practice and to his games, carrying Ramon's equipment bag. "Just to see professional ballplayers in the Dominican was special," Pedro later said. "But to be on the same field was a dream. I used to dream that one day, my brothers and I would be in the major leagues together."[17]

Pedro was smaller than Ramon—at the time he only weighed about 135 pounds—but he could throw a ball almost as hard. He played in games around town, where he was considered a tough, scrappy competitor. One day, a pitching coach in Santo Domingo saw Pedro playing on the sidelines, and he was impressed with the young boy's fastball. He told Pedro that, like his older brother, he, too, could be a professional baseball player if he worked hard and dedicated himself to the game.

The next year, Ramon was called up to the Dodgers' Class A team in Bakersfield, California. With the help of Ralph Avila, Ramon was bulking up, getting stronger, and improving his technique. The next season, he moved to another Dodgers team, in Vero Beach, Florida, and then in 1988 he was sent up to the Class AA team, the San Antonio Missions. Ramon soon became one of the top pitchers in the Texas League, and by the end of the season he was called up to the major leagues. Ramon pitched in nine games for the league-leading Los Angeles

Ramon Martinez, Pedro's eldest brother, was signed by the Los Angeles Dodgers in 1984 at the age of 16. After four years in the minor leagues, Ramon made his major league debut in 1988 and is pictured here tossing the lone no-hitter of his career—a 7-0 win over the Florida Marlins on July 14, 1995.

Dodgers, helping the team in their successful pursuit of the 1988 World Series title.

Dodgers manager Tommy Lasorda, however, thought Ramon Martinez needed a bit more seasoning, and in the beginning of 1989 he sent the young pitcher back to the Class AAA team, the Albuquerque Dukes. But Ramon soon proved his mettle and was back in the majors, finishing the year with the Dodgers in Los Angeles.

In 1990, Ramon came into his own, as he developed into a star pitcher for the Dodgers. He threw a memorable shutout against the Atlanta Braves on June 4, striking out 18 batters, which tied a team record for most strikeouts in one game. Ramon was selected as a pitcher for the National League All-Star team that year. He finished the season with a 20-6 record and a 2.92 ERA.

For all his success, Ramon did not forget his little brother. "I'd love to play with him, give him advice," Ramon told *Sports Illustrated*. "I can teach him little things. He'll show me his change-up and I'll say, 'Here's how I throw mine.'"[18]

In 1988, Ramon helped 16-year-old Pedro win his own contract with the Dodgers. For the next two seasons, Pedro worked with coaches in the Dominican Republic and played in a league with other teenaged prospects. While he trained, Pedro also attended school in Santo Domingo. Pedro was a good student, especially interested in studying English—for he was determined, like his brother, to make his way up the baseball ranks and get to the United States.

Soon enough, in 1990, the Dodgers called Pedro up to their rookie team in Great Falls, Montana, where the young pitcher made an immediate impact. He struck out 82 batters that season, working in 77 innings, and posted a won-lost record of 8-3. Pedro was named to the rookie league's All-Star team.

The next year, 1991, Pedro moved up to the Class A team in Bakersfield, California—the same town where his brother Ramon had once played. Pedro started in ten games and boasted an 8-0 record. While he was with the Bakersfield team, Pedro's ERA was a miserly 2.05—one of the best in the league.

The Dodgers saw promise in Pedro and were particularly impressed by his smooth, compact motion that generated a surprising amount of speed. They soon sent him up to the Class AA team in San Antonio, Texas, where he recorded an amazingly low ERA of 1.76. Except for the new star pitcher, though, the San Antonio Missions did not make for much of a squad. The batters didn't drive in many runs, and so Pedro only won two more games than he lost. Still, the Dodgers realized they had a hot prospect. Before the 1991 season was even over, they pushed Pedro up yet another level, to the Albuquerque Dukes, the same Class AAA team where Ramon had been pitching two years before.

Pedro pitched in six games for the Dukes and finished the 1991 season with a total record of 18-8, generating a 2.28 ERA and 192 strikeouts. *The Sporting News*, a weekly national sports magazine, named Pedro its Minor League Player of the Year.

The promising pitcher was hoping to get to the major leagues in 1992. But the Dodgers felt he needed more time to prove himself, so Pedro went back to the Albuquerque Dukes. His ERA floated up to 3.81—in part because he suffered from some shoulder problems—but he struck out a team-leading 124 batters and was selected for the AAA All-Star Game.

At the end of the summer, the Dodgers finally gave Pedro a call, and the 20-year-old Dominican joined his brother Ramon on the Dodgers' pitching staff. In his first outing, September 24, 1992, Pedro was called to pitch in relief against the Cincinnati Reds and threw two scoreless innings. The following week, Pedro was tapped to start a game against the Reds.

As his brother watched from the Dodgers' bench, Pedro took the mound. The first batter hit a ground-rule double off the rookie and later came in to score a run. Pedro gave up a second run in the third inning. But then he retired ten batters in a row to finish off six innings of respectable pitching (although the Reds eventually won the game, 3-1). "I wasn't nervous out there, I was very confident," recalled Martinez. "I knew what I wanted to do and I did it, for the most part. They got some hits and a few runs, but overall it went well."[19]

Added Dodgers manager Tommy Lasorda, "He had great command. We liked what we saw in spring training and we really liked what we saw tonight. He could really be a good one."[20]

Pedro's dream had come true. He was in the majors, pitching alongside his brother, the star hurler of the team. And now with the season over, both Pedro and Ramon returned to the Dominican Republic. Pedro had to go to the doctor for minor surgery to correct the problem in his arm. After some rehabilitation, he focused his attention on getting ready for the 1993 season. He was going to the Dodgers' spring training camp—and he desperately wanted to stay on the team.

3

A Real Major Leaguer

At the beginning of the 1993 season, Pedro traveled to Florida to report to Dodgers spring training. He pitched impressively, but manager Tommy Lasorda decided to send Pedro back to Albuquerque for some additional seasoning. Pedro was furious about Lasorda's decision, and even thought about quitting the game and going home. But his brother Ramon, now the Dodgers' ace, reminded him that he, too, had been sent back to the minor leagues early in his career. If Ramon could pitch his way over this hurdle, then so could his younger brother.

Pedro packed his bags, moved back to Albuquerque, and took the mound for the opening game of the Duke's season. He was pitching in the third inning—and had already struck out four batters—when the telephone rang at the stadium. The Dodgers were on the line. One of their relief pitchers was injured. They needed Pedro to return to Los Angeles right away. The Albuquerque pitching

34

Pedro Martinez made his major league debut with the Los Angeles Dodgers on September 24, 1992, pitching two innings of scoreless relief in an 8-4 loss to the Cincinnati Reds. Martinez, pictured here pitching against the New York Mets in 1993, spent a little more than a season with the Dodgers before being traded to the Montreal Expos in November 1993.

coach marched to the mound, pulled Pedro out of the game, and told him he was going back to Los Angeles.

"I spent the whole day unpacking," Martinez recalled. "At night I packed it all up again."[21]

But Martinez didn't mind, because this time he was in the big leagues for good. The Dodgers put him in the bullpen as a reliever. In his first game of the 1993 season—only a day after he'd left Albuquerque—the 21-year-old Pedro came in to relieve his 25-year-old brother Ramon, who'd started the game against the Atlanta Braves. According to Pedro, it was the first time he had ever pitched in the same game as Ramon. Why? "He was always too far ahead of me," admitted the younger Martinez.[22]

Unfortunately, Dodger bats went cold that day, and Los Angeles lost the game. But soon after that, Pedro showed his first flash of pitching genius. It was April 28, 1993, and the Dodgers were playing at home against the Montreal Expos. Los Angeles was ahead 3-1 in the seventh inning. Montreal was batting. With no outs and a man on first, manager Tommy Lasorda called for Pedro to pitch in relief. The first batter hit a single to left, putting men on first and second. The winning run stepped up to the plate.

Pedro glared at him, reared back, and threw a strike. The next pitch sailed in, and the batter fouled it off for strike two. Then Pedro breezed another one by for a strikeout, to get the first out of the inning.

Montreal infielder Delino DeShields stepped up to bat. Pedro struck him out. No problem. Two outs.

Then Moises Alou, son of Expos manager Felipe Alou, came to the plate. The future All-Star checked his swing, squirted a slow grounder to third base, and raced to first. He was safe. The two other runners advanced. The bases were loaded. Two away.

Up came another Montreal All-Star, outfielder Marquis Grissom. Pedro threw a strike. Then another. Pedro's next three pitches missed the plate, bringing the count to 3-2.

Pedro dealt the next pitch. Grissom took a swing . . . strike three! The young Dominican had gotten the Dodgers out of a jam, with no runs scored, showing he could perform in a pressure situation, as his team held on to win the game.

Pedro garnered some attention for this performance, and as the 1993 season went on, the young hurler started to hit his stride, finding a regular spot as a reliever for the Dodgers. He also began to put up some winning numbers. During that summer, he won eight games in a row. He chalked up 119 strikeouts in the 109 innings he pitched, and posted a 2.61 ERA—impressive for any pitcher, much less a rookie. His presence on the mound also helped the Dodgers improve their record. The previous year, 1992, they had come in at the bottom of the standings in the National League West. In 1993, they moved up to third place.

As Pedro and Ramon went home to prepare for the 1994 season, however, manager Tommy Lasorda mulled over some possible changes to his lineup. Dodger coaches wondered about Pedro's staying power. Sure he was good. But at only five foot eleven and now 160 pounds, was he strong enough to carry a full pitching load for the season? They finally decided to trade him to the Montreal Expos for second baseman Delino DeShields, who despite having struck out against Pedro in the seventh inning of that April game, was a good-fielding, good-hitting infielder who had batted .295 the previous season.

At first, both Ramon and Pedro were disappointed that Pedro was leaving. They liked being on the same team. Also, Montreal was not much of a team. The Expos could not afford to pay top players, and the results were predictable: The Expos were perennial also-rans that had never won a regular-season pennant.

But the move also presented an opportunity for Pedro. "It made me sad when he was traded," explained Ramon. "But I was also happy because the role he had with the Dodgers was in the bullpen. In Montreal he would get to be a starter."[23]

Added Pedro himself: "I am a starter. The Dodgers asked me to be a reliever. That was an adjustment because I was always a starter in the minor leagues. The fact I did well as a reliever I think shows that I'm a good pitcher. But now I'm a starter again. That's what I've always been. This is natural for me."[24]

Unfortunately, the 1994 season did not begin well for either Pedro or the Expos. Pedro pitched in their home opener against the Chicago Cubs, and the Expos lost, 4-0. On April 13, Pedro entered the eighth inning against the Cincinnati Reds pitching a perfect game (no hits, no walks), but then he hit Reggie Sanders on the elbow with a fastball. Although everyone agreed Pedro didn't do it on purpose—what pitcher wants to give up a perfect game?—Sanders took offense, charged the mound, and tackled Martinez while teammates rushed out to join the brawl. The umpires ejected Sanders from the field, and

BEING HISPANIC

THE DOMINICAN DANDY'S INFLUENCE ON PEDRO

When Pedro Martinez won his first Cy Young Award in 1997, he gave credit to a boyhood hero. "I'm dedicating this award to Juan Marichal," he announced, "who I think deserved this award and didn't get it."*

The Dominican Dandy—as Marichal was known in his heyday, partly for his tall, thin appearance and his high-kick delivery—was then 60 years old, and he worked as the Secretary of Sports for the Dominican Republic. Marichal had pitched in the majors from 1960 to 1975—primarily for the San Francisco Giants, and then, briefly, for the Boston Red Sox and the Los Angeles Dodgers. Marichal won 243 games during his career, including 20 or more games in six seasons for the Giants.

Earlier in 1997, Juan Marichal had traveled to Montreal and watched Pedro earn a victory against his old team. "I really like his style, he's very aggressive," Marichal commented about the younger Dominican. "He's not afraid to pitch, in and out. I think that was my style. I loved to pitch inside. Pedro, he has no fear. He knows how to pitch, even at his age. Sometimes it takes longer to become a good pitcher, but he has improved every year. And he has a better change-up than the one I threw."**

Even though Marichal had played in Boston for only half a season at

Montreal won the game. But Pedro, who made no secret of his strategy of brushing back batters with inside pitches, was beginning to develop a reputation as a guy who threw at hitters, perhaps even on purpose. Sports reporters began calling him "Señor Plunk."

Manager Felipe Alou, though, stood behind his new starter. He said that Pedro reminded him of another Dominican pitcher he'd known when he was growing up:

the end of his career, he liked the city. Marichal's daughter went to graduate school at Boston University, and when Pedro was being courted by the Red Sox, Marichal encouraged him to put on a Boston uniform. Whatever success Boston would later enjoy, Marichal was partly responsible.

Juan Marichal was elected into the Baseball Hall of Fame in 1983, but during his career he never won the Cy Young Award. On January 23, 1998, he had the honor of presenting the award to Pedro Martinez at a dinner in Boston. Pedro bowed in deference to the older pitcher and told him, "You are my daddy." Pedro embraced his hero. He then held out the award and gave it to Marichal.

"Pedro, I know how you feel," Marichal responded, insisting Pedro keep the award for himself. "I know how I feel. But this belongs to you. You deserve it."***

  * "P. Martinez Wins NL Cy Young," *Washington Post*, November 11, 1997; also: Ronald Blum, "Cy Young One Week; Traded the Next," Associated Press, in *York* (PA) *Daily Record*, November 12, 1997.

 ** Gordon Edes, "Marichal Put in Good Word with Martinez—Former Sox Righthander Speaks Very Highly of Team, City," *Boston Globe*, December 16, 1997.

*** Edes, "Martinez Gets Cy, Gives It to Marichal," *Boston Globe*, January 23, 1998.

Juan Marichal, the Dominican right-hander who was a star with the San Francisco Giants in the 1960s and early 1970s. "He's similar to Juan Marichal, along the lines of presentation—fearless and challenging," Alou told *USA Today*. "He's a young, skinny kid throwing 95-miles-per-hour fastballs inside on the plate. Batters don't like that. You have to be tough. If you're small, you've got to be tougher."[25]

By the beginning of August, the Expos were surprising everyone by leading their division in the National League, with a chance at getting to the World Series. But that was a year of unrest in baseball, and on August 12 the players' union went on strike. The remainder of the season was canceled. No division playoffs. No league championships. For the first time since 1904, no World Series.

Despite the strike, however, Felipe Alou was named manager of the year by the Associated Press and *The Sporting News*, and everyone agreed Pedro made an outstanding debut as a starting pitcher. He posted an 11-5 record, with 142 strikeouts and an ERA of 3.42.

Pedro was on his way.

BROTHER VERSUS BROTHER

After their surprisingly good showing in 1994, expectations were high for the Expos in 1995. But that year, disappointment ruled in Montreal. The season started late because of the strike; and when play did begin, Montreal was at a disadvantage. The team had traded away its three highest-paid players (outfielders Larry Walker and Marquis Grissom, and pitcher Ken Hill), and so while it saved some $10 million in payroll, it lost any chance at competing for postseason play.

Even so, Pedro Martinez held up his end on the mound. He started out by beating the Pittsburgh Pirates and the New York Mets. He pitched his way through nine perfect innings on June 3 against the San Diego Padres—retiring 27 batters in a row. Unfortunately, the Expos could score no runs for Pedro, so the

Pedro Martinez spent four seasons in Montreal (1994–97), where he posted a record of 55-33 and an earned run average of 3.13. During the strike-shortened 1994 season, the Expos went 74-40 but were just 232-236 over the next three years.

game went into extra innings, and Pedro gave up a double in the tenth. No one scored, and Montreal went on to get a run in the bottom of the tenth, to win the game, 1-0. Although Pedro got the win with a shutout, he was robbed of his perfect game.

By season's end, Pedro was 14-10. It was the best pitching performance on a team that limped in with a record of 74 wins and 88 losses. Pedro also boasted 174 strikeouts in the shortened season, with a respectable ERA of 3.51.

The next year, Pedro started where he'd left off. He pitched a two-hitter against the Mets on May 1. He struck out 11 Cincinnati Reds on June 14. And for the first time, Pedro was chosen to go to the All-Star Game, as a member of the National League pitching staff, where he allowed two hits but no runs in contributing to his team's 6-0 victory.

The highlight of the 1996 season, though, came on August 29. The Montreal Expos and the Los Angeles Dodgers were scheduled to play each other in Montreal. The two teams were vying for the wild-card spot to get into the National League playoffs.

Pedro Martinez, with an 11-8 record, was slated to start for the Expos. Ramon Martinez, with a 10-6 record, was tapped to begin the game for the Dodgers. Pedro said he asked manager Felipe Alou to juggle the pitching rotation. He didn't want to have a showdown against his brother. "We're too close. We're like the same person," said Pedro. "If I had to give up my career to help my brother go on, I would do it. That's the reason I am here, because of Ramon."[26]

But no changes were in the offing. The two brothers took the mound against each other.

The first two innings were scoreless. In the bottom of the third, the Expos came up. Pedro was first to bat. Ramon got his brother to fly out to right field.

Then the Expo center fielder hit a high chopper to third base and made it to first for a single. Ramon went on to walk the next three batters and force in the first Expo run. The bases were still loaded, with only one out. Ramon got the next Expo hitter to pop out to third, and the one after that grounded to first. Ramon finished the inning, allowing only one run.

Pedro cruised through the first three innings. But in the fourth, with the Expos ahead, 1-0, Mike Piazza, the Dodger catcher, came up to bat. With a 3-2 count, Piazza stroked a ball into the stands for a home run to tie the game. Two pitches later, Dodger first baseman Eric Karros hit another homer over the left-field wall—back-to-back home runs against Pedro—to put the Dodgers in front, 2-1.

Ramon did not allow a hit to the next 18 Expo batters, and the game ended with the Dodgers on top, 2-1. Ramon struck out seven, walked five, and allowed three hits. Pedro struck out 12 batters, but the two home runs were his undoing in what everyone considered an excellent, if losing, performance. "It's a shame someone had to lose that game," said Ramon's teammate Mike Piazza. "Fortunately for us, it was the younger brother."[27]

As for Ramon, he was simply relieved at the outcome. "Once I got out of that inning, I took a deep breath and pitched well," he said. "I don't feel sorry for Pedro, because he did a great job and could have won."[28]

Ramon went on to sum up: "I'm very proud of the job that Pedro did. It was a very big challenge for both of us. When he left the mound in the ninth, I made a sign to him to tell him that I love him and that he pitched a great game . . . I just wanted to go out and win and put us back in the wild-card lead. It was a great game, and I'm glad it's over."[29]

When Pedro left the mound in the ninth inning, he received a standing ovation from the Montreal crowd. Later, he said of his brother: "He's been a great example to me my whole life . . . he's always been there for me. He taught me how to play baseball and he's taught me about life. He's my idol. It was a little different preparing for this game because I had to go up there thinking that I was going to defeat my brother or that he was going to defeat me. It was hard and it will never be easy if it happens again because it's blood against blood and it's the same blood. I was happy to see the crowd give him such a good hand. It's nice to see that they liked him as much as they liked me."[30]

A few weeks later, Pedro finished the year with a 13-10 record. He posted an ERA of 3.70—a good average for an ordinary pitcher but disappointing for a star like Pedro. Furthermore, he got into another brawl that marred the end of the season. In a September 24 game against the Philadelphia Phillies, Pedro hit a batter in the third inning. When Pedro

THE CY YOUNG AWARD

Cy Young was a right-handed pitcher who played in the late 1800s and the early 1900s, and won 511 games, more than any other pitcher in the history of baseball. In his 22-year major league career, he boasted 16 seasons when he won 20 games or more—and five seasons when he won 30 games or more. Born and raised in Ohio, his real name was Denton True Young. He got the nickname "Cy" because people thought he threw his fastball like a cyclone.

Cy Young spent several years in Cleveland, and then St. Louis, before moving to Boston in 1901, for a—get this—$600 raise! He spent eight years in Boston, then went back to Cleveland, then returned to Boston to finish out his career. In all, he pitched 74 shutouts, including three no-hitters and one perfect game. He was elected to the Baseball Hall of Fame in 1937.

The Cy Young Award, presented annually, was introduced in 1956 to honor the great baseball pioneer who had passed away the previous year at the age of 88. Through 1966, just one Cy Young was awarded each year, to the best pitcher in baseball. Since 1967, two awards have been given, one to the best pitcher in each league.

then came up to bat in the fifth, the Phillies' pitcher threw an inside pitch, as Pedro skipped out of the way. Then the next pitch went behind Pedro's back.

Pedro thought the pitcher was throwing at him on purpose. He ran to the mound, helmet in hand. He swung the helmet at the pitcher, then the two tumbled to the ground as both teams ran out onto the field to defend their teammates. The umpires took several minutes to settle things down, and

Recent Cy Young Winners:

	National League	*American League*
1995	Greg Maddux Atlanta Braves	Randy Johnson Seattle Mariners
1996	John Smoltz Atlanta Braves	Pat Hentgen Toronto Blue Jays
1997	Pedro Martinez Montreal Expos	Roger Clemens Toronto Blue Jays
1998	Tom Glavine Atlanta Braves	Roger Clemens Toronto Blue Jays
1999	Randy Johnson Arizona Diamondbacks	Pedro Martinez Boston Red Sox
2000	Randy Johnson Arizona Diamondbacks	Pedro Martinez Boston Red Sox
2001	Randy Johnson Arizona Diamondbacks	Roger Clemens New York Yankees
2002	Randy Johnson Arizona Diamondbacks	Barry Zito Oakland Athletics
2003	Eric Gagne Los Angeles Dodgers	Roy Halladay Toronto Blue Jays
2004	Roger Clemens Houston Astros	Johan Santana Minnesota Twins
2005	Chris Carpenter St. Louis Cardinals	Bartolo Colon Los Angeles Angels

they ejected both Martinez and the Philadelphia pitcher from the game. Pedro was ultimately given an eight-game suspension.

With his season over, Pedro went back to the Dominican Republic. He was determined to do better the next year. Indeed, 1997 was the season that brought Pedro to the pinnacle. He had to sit out the first two weeks of the season, because the suspension was carried over from the previous year. But when he finally did start pitching, on April 15, he won his first game against the Houston Astros. Then he pitched a shutout against the San Diego Padres and another against the New York Mets.

At that point, he was off and running, playing in the All-Star Game, vying for the Cy Young Award. When the year was finished, he became only the fifth pitcher in National League history to strike out more than 300 batters in a season. Opponents managed a skimpy .184 batting average against him—the lowest average against any major league pitcher that year—and despite his team's scoring struggles, Pedro managed to finish with a 17-8 won-lost record.

It was that November, after all the votes were counted, when he was named *The Sporting News* National League Pitcher of the Year and then was selected as the 1997 National League Cy Young Award winner.

Then in December, Pedro pocketed his big payoff, as the Expos traded him to Boston. In return, the Expos got two other pitchers, Carl Pavano and Tony Armas, Jr. Pedro, of course, got his record-setting contract, and the chance to play in a town where baseball is king.

Pedro could have signed with the Red Sox for just one year and kept his options open after the 1998 season. The Red Sox, however, wanted him to stay awhile, so they reached deep and came up with that fat contract that would pay him $75 million, keeping him in Boston for at least six years. At the time, at the end of 1997, it made Pedro the highest-paid player in all of baseball.

Beyond the money, Pedro knew Boston had a better team than Montreal. Boston hitters would give him more support, allowing him to post better won-lost records—and perhaps, after six years in the major leagues, give him a chance to play in the postseason championships.

So Pedro was bound for Boston.

Best Pitcher in the Game

Pedro went to Boston with much fanfare and posted a successful season in 1998, which culminated in a playoff berth against the Cleveland Indians. The Red Sox had not made it to the World Series, but Pedro finally *did* make it to a championship series and won his first postseason game, even if his team faltered.

Meanwhile, his brother Ramon had run into a problem. The Dodgers' pitching ace sustained an injury in June 1998 in a game against the Colorado Rockies, tearing the rotator cuff in his right shoulder. He was sidelined for the rest of the season.

In 1998, Ramon was in the fourth year of a four-year contract. The Dodgers had the option to renew for a year, but in October management announced that instead of paying the injured Martinez $5.6 million to play baseball, the team would give him $600,000 to buy out the option. Ramon was a free agent—free to sign a deal with any team he wanted, and that wanted him.

At the end of 1998, Ramon and Pedro went home to the

Dominican Republic for the winter. Ramon wasn't too worried about securing another contract. Instead, he focused on getting his arm better. When he heard that there was interest from the Boston Red Sox, though, Ramon signaled that he was ready to go. He would love another chance to play with his brother.

In March 1999, Ramon signed a two-year deal with the Red Sox, with an option for a third year. The contract was reportedly worth $7 million for the first two years—not as much as his younger brother was making but still a *lot* of money!

However, Ramon's shoulder continued to sideline him. He spent most of the summer of 1999 recuperating, warming up, getting ready, and trying out his arm in the Red Sox minor league system. He didn't pitch for the Red Sox until September, when he only threw a few innings in a couple of games.

While Ramon stumbled, Pedro only got stronger. He started out his second season with the Red Sox by pitching the opening game against the Royals, on a windy April day in Kansas City. Pedro gave up a home run, plus another run, in the very first inning. But that shaky start was not a harbinger of things to come. Pedro went on to win that opening game against the Royals, 5-3. A week later, the Red Sox won their fifth game in a row—the first five games of the season—when Pedro beat the Tampa Bay Devil Rays.

By the All-Star Game on July 13, Pedro boasted a 15-3 record, with a 2.10 ERA and 184 strikeouts. Manager Jimy Williams was astounded by the talent of his pitcher. "Do you people realize what you're seeing?" he asked the sportswriters. "Do you realize how special this young man is and how special it is what he's doing?"[31]

Pedro was selected as the American League All-Star starting pitcher by Joe Torre, the Yankee manager who was leading the All-Star team that year. The game would take place on Pedro's home field of Fenway Park.

In the 1999 All-Star Game at Boston's Fenway Park, Pedro Martinez was named the game's Most Valuable Player after leading the American League to a 4-1 win over the National League. Martinez, who is pictured here holding the MVP trophy above his head, pitched two scoreless innings, allowed no hits, and struck out five batters.

Pedro started the game by striking out National League All-Stars Barry Larkin and Larry Walker. Then up stepped slugger Sammy Sosa. Pedro struck him out—Sosa swung at a fastball and missed, to end the first inning.

In the second inning, National League home run king Mark McGwire led off, and . . . you guessed it, Pedro struck him out! Then Matt Williams reached first base on an error by the second baseman; but Pedro struck out the next batter as Williams got caught stealing for an inning-ending double play.

The American League won the contest, 4-1, and Pedro was named Most Valuable Player of the game. "He's got three devastating pitches," said an awestruck Mark McGwire, the National League first baseman and one of Pedro's strikeout victims. "What can you say? He's the best pitcher in the game."[32]

The Red Sox, with their fast start to the season, and enjoying the benefits of "the best pitcher in the game," were winning more games than anyone had expected—they were in the thick of the race for the American League pennant. By the beginning of September, Boston was in second place in the American League East division, trying to catch the Yankees, while fighting off the Toronto Blue Jays and the surging Oakland Athletics for the wild-card spot in the playoffs.

Pedro sat out for a couple of weeks in August, because of a sore shoulder, but on September 3, he posted a victory over the Seattle Mariners to win his twentieth game and become the first 20-game winner of the 1999 season in the major leagues. It was also Pedro's first 20-win season—and the first time a Red Sox pitcher had reached that milestone since Roger Clemens went 21-6 for Boston in 1990.

On September 10, the Red Sox traveled to Yankee Stadium, $6^1/_2$ games behind the league-leading Bronx Bombers. That day, according to the *New York Times*, Pedro Martinez "humbled the Yankees in their home park in a manner never seen before."[33]

Pedro struck out 17 Yankees, the most ever against this ball club, without giving up a walk. He struck out every batter at least once. He allowed only one hit—a home run by Chili Davis in the second inning—and won the game, 3-1.

Puzzled Yankee batters admired Pedro's performance, pointing to his spinning curveball that circled in for strikes, his jumping 97-mile-an-hour fastball, and the change-up that looked so tantalizing until it seemed to drop out of sight. "That is about as unhittable as you can find," said Yankee manager Joe Torre. "You can't fault the hitters."[34]

As Pedro racked up the strikeouts—a career high—the Yankee fans among the 55,000 people in the stadium could do nothing but admire Pedro's performance. But the Boston fans in right field hung cards bearing the letter "K" to keep count. Pedro ended the game by striking out the last five batters and eight of the last nine.

"I've never seen anyone pitch like he did tonight," said Ramon, his older brother. "And I've seen guys pitch perfect games, no hitters."[35]

Commented manager Jimy Williams: "He's the best pitcher in baseball right now. Anyone knows that. . . . Tonight all three of his pitches were working, he threw all of them for strikes. When he is like that he can pitch with his eyes closed."[36]

Pedro's season wasn't over, though, not by a long shot.

On September 27, Pedro pitched a 5-3 victory over the Baltimore Orioles to ensure Boston at least a tie for the wild-card spot. To cap off the season, on October 2, Pedro's brother Ramon pitched six shutout innings against the Orioles. Then Pedro entered the game in the seventh inning in relief of his brother—the first time they had pitched together on the same team since that day in Los Angeles six years before.

The Red Sox finished the season in second place, with a 94-68 record, four games behind the Yankees but comfortably ahead of the Oakland Athletics for the wild-card spot. Before they played the Yankees for the American League championship, however, the Red Sox first had to get past the Cleveland Indians in the division series—the very team that had beaten them in the 1998 ALDS.

Once again optimism ruled in Red Sox Nation. The last

time the Red Sox had made two consecutive postseason appearances was back in 1915 and 1916. The last time the Red Sox won the World Series was in 1918. Boston fans couldn't help but wonder: Could the Red Sox go all the way this year? Could they close out the century by bringing back the trophy that had last been in Boston 81 years before? Perhaps "the curse of the Bambino" would finally be broken in 1991.

THE PLAYOFFS

Pedro started the first game in Cleveland for the best-of-five ALDS against the Indians. The Boston plan: Pedro would pitch twice and win, and somehow the Red Sox would take another game to capture the series.

The Boston plan blew up in the fourth inning of Game 1. Pedro struck out the first Cleveland batter with a fastball. Then . . . "I felt a burning sensation in my back,"[37] said Pedro. He got the next two batters out—but he knew something was wrong. So did everyone else, as his fastball was suddenly registering less than 90 miles an hour, instead of the usual 95 to 98 miles an hour. Apparently, Pedro had pulled a muscle under his right shoulder. It wasn't too serious, medically speaking. But it was very serious for the Red Sox, as their last best hope had to hit the shower.

Pedro left the game with a 2-0 lead, but it didn't take long for the Indians to start their comeback. They tied the game with a two-run homer in the sixth inning. In the ninth inning, the Indians loaded the bases, with only one out. Cleveland infielder Travis Fryman then lined a single to left to bring in the winning run.

So Cleveland took the first game, 3-2. "We got a break with Pedro getting hurt," admitted Fryman. "Any time you face Pedro, he's tough. He's the best pitcher I ever faced. You look up there in the sixth inning and you don't see him out there, it gives you a little pick-me-up."[38]

In Game 2, the Red Sox went with veteran pitcher Bret Saberhagen, who got bombed for six runs in the third inning.

The Indians went on to humiliate Boston with an 11-1 victory. By the time the Red Sox came home to Fenway Park, they were down 2-0 in the series, one game away from being eliminated. Their backs were against the wall.

Manager Jimy Williams decided to go with Ramon for the next game, hoping for six good innings from the recently recuperating older Martinez. On October 9, 1999, Ramon started Game 3. He pitched his way into the sixth inning, allowing two runs, as his brother Pedro sat in the dugout coaching him, giving him pointers, urging him on. "I talked to him all the time,"[39] said Pedro with a grin. The pep talk worked, as Boston ended up on top, 9-3. The Red Sox were still alive.

THE CURSE OF THE BAMBINO

Back in the early 1900s, Boston fielded the best team in baseball, winning the World Series five times. But in 1920, Boston traded its star player, George Herman Ruth—also known as Babe Ruth, or The Bambino—to the New York Yankees.

Up until 1920, the Yankees had never won the World Series. But between 1920 and 2004, New York won the World Series 26 times. Boston, meanwhile, which last won in 1918, never won again. That's the Curse of the Bambino.

The Red Sox have come close—but each time they have fallen short, sometimes in agonizing ways. In 1946, 1967, and 1975, they went to the World Series and lost in seven games.

In 1978, in July, the Red Sox enjoyed a 14-game lead over the Yankees for the American League pennant. But they collapsed. Oh, did they collapse. By the end of the season, the two teams were tied. There would be a one-game playoff. Going into the seventh, the Red Sox were ahead, 2-0. Up came Yankee shortstop Bucky Dent, an average hitter, and he launched a ball over Fenway's Green Monster in left field for a three-run homer.

The fourth game, in Boston, turned into a slugfest for the Red Sox, as they beat the Indians 23-7. Boston set a record for most runs in a postseason victory. Now, back from the brink, the Red Sox were going to Cleveland for the final game. With the series tied 2-2, everyone in Boston wanted to know: How was Pedro's back? Could he pitch in the fifth and deciding game?

"It feels much better," Pedro reported. "I feel I can pitch soon, but it's not up to me when I pitch. It's up to the manager when I pitch again."[40]

Jimy Williams soon gave the answer. He scheduled Bret Saberhagen to start in Cleveland.

Boston scored two runs in the first inning to take a quick

With that Bucky Dent home run went Red Sox dreams for the championship.

The next time victory dangled in front of the Red Sox was in 1986. Boston made it to the World Series against the New York Mets. The Red Sox went into Game 6 of that series with a 3-2 lead. One more win and the crown was theirs.

Boston took the lead early in Game 6, but the Mets caught up. Boston went ahead again, and the Mets caught up. The game was tied after nine innings. In the bottom of the tenth, a Mets ground ball rolled to Boston first baseman Bill Buckner. It was a routine grounder, but Buckner let the ball squirt between his legs. Instead of Boston getting the inning-ending out, the Mets scored a run from second base—and won the game.

The Mets went on to win Game 7, and the World Series, once again denying the Red Sox the victory they so craved—the Bill Buckner moment came to symbolize eight decades of Red Sox anguish and frustration.

And as the new millennium dawned, the legend lived on . . . Babe, Bucky, Buckner. Would the curse ever end?

lead, but Saberhagen was hit hard by the Indians. He gave up five runs before leaving the game in the second inning.

Boston pitcher Derek Lowe relieved Saberhagen in the second and got the Indians out. The next inning, Boston scored a run to make it 5-3. Then Boston's left fielder, Troy O'Leary, smashed a grand slam home run into the right-field stands to put Boston ahead by a score of 7-5.

The Indians came up again, and they brought three more runs across the plate to go ahead 8-7. The Red Sox responded with one more, to tie the game at 8-8. At that point, Boston manager Jimy Williams signaled to the bullpen. Was he calling Pedro?

Williams didn't want to risk hurting his star pitcher—but he desperately needed someone to save the season, and Pedro claimed he was ready. No matter that he had been hurt. No matter that he was now a starting pitcher, not a reliever. This was no time to stand on ceremony. The Red Sox needed him.

So Pedro walked onto the field. Williams said later he'd decided he would use Pedro for just an inning or two—to stop the Cleveland momentum. Then he would turn to someone else.

"I had doubts until I stepped out onto the mound," said Pedro. "Once I did, I never did. I threw four or five pitches and felt pretty good. I just wanted to get the adrenaline going and the mind going. I couldn't push myself to throw the fastball as fast as I could. So I just laid the ball over, made good pitches and hit the spots."[41]

Pedro pitched that fourth inning masterfully. Then he pitched another. He didn't allow even one hit. Pedro told Williams he felt strong.

"I decided I was going to be out there and whatever happened, happened," Pedro later reflected. "If they decided to take me out in the middle of an inning, I would do that, but I had to be out there as long as I could."[42]

Pedro got the Indians out in the sixth inning. In the top of the seventh, Boston's Troy O'Leary again came through, hitting a three-run homer. Now the Red Sox were ahead, 11-8. Could Pedro hold on?

"It felt a little tighter in the last two innings," Pedro later revealed. "But the adrenaline at that point, and knowing that we had the lead and I had to make sure we kept the lead, I guess I was getting a little stronger. I wasn't going to let go."[43]

The Red Sox scored another run in the top of the ninth. Then Pedro closed out the game, getting three straight outs, including a strikeout of the last Cleveland batter. In all, Pedro nursed his arm through six innings, striking out eight batters and not allowing one hit. It was a Martinez miracle as the Red Sox put away the game, 12-8, making an incredible comeback to win the series, 3-2.

"We've got a lot of heart on this team," said Troy O'Leary. "Pedro showed it. He pitched like the Cy Young winner he is."[44]

Added Boston pitching coach Joe Kerrigan: "It's one of the most heroic, gutsy performances I've ever seen. Here's a guy who wasn't supposed to pitch tonight except for an inning or two. And here he is throwing a hundred pitches." Kerrigan marveled, "The legend of Pedro."[45]

But even as the champagne flowed in the Boston club-house, the powerful Yankees lurked around the corner—for with that victory in Cleveland, the Red Sox had won a ticket to New York and the chance to play the defending World Series champion Yankees for the ALCS. And Pedro—he'd just pitched six innings. He wouldn't be ready to take the mound again until Game 3 against the Yankees.

A tired Boston team jetted to New York to meet the Bronx Bombers. The Red Sox got off to a good start in Game 1, scoring two runs in the first inning, and another in the second, to surge ahead, 3-0. But the Yankees tied it up, 3-3, in the seventh, and after nine innings the game was still tied at 3-3.

Boston failed to score in its half of the tenth. Then the Yankees came up, and outfielder Bernie Williams hit a long fly ball that sailed over the center-field fence. A home run. The Yankees won it, the first game of the series, by a score of 4-3.

The tall, thin older brother was tapped by Boston to start Game 2. Ramon Martinez worked his way through six innings, allowing only one run, while Boston's Nomar Garciaparra hit a two-run homer in the fifth to put the Red Sox ahead, 2-1.

Once again, Boston hopes were raised, but in the seventh inning, Ramon walked the lead-off hitter. Then a double brought in a run. Martinez was relieved, but the fresh arm let Yankee Paul O'Neill loop a single to left to score another run. The Red Sox, down 3-2, put men on base in the ninth inning but failed to score, and lost the game to fall behind 2-0 in the series.

Boston had been down to the Cleveland Indians, 2-0, and had made a comeback. Could they do it against the power-house Yankees? It would be up to Pedro, who was slated to pitch in Game 3 against Roger Clemens, the former Red Sox ace who had spent 13 years in Boston dazzling the fans, but who had left for Toronto and now belonged to the Yankees. The same Roger Clemens who was a five-time Cy Young Award winner—who had outpolled Pedro in the Cy Young race just the previous season.

The duel between Pedro Martinez, age 27, and Roger Clemens, age 37, was billed as "The Game of the Century" in Boston. A sign on a main thoroughfare, Storrow Drive, that originally read "Reverse Curve" was changed to read "Reverse the Curse." It was a battle between the aging veteran and the young upstart. One Boston bumper sticker labeled it: Cy Young versus Cy Old.

Pedro took the mound in the fist inning amidst chants of "Pe-dro!" "Pe-dro!" Still a little sore from his bout with the Cleveland Indians, Pedro did not have his usual speed on the fastball. It was registering at 88 to 90 miles an hour, instead of his usual 95 to 98 miles an hour. "In the first inning I had exactly what I had the whole game—nothing," Pedro admitted. "I had to pretty much mix up my pitches and try to catch them guessing wrong and hit the spots. That was the key, hitting the spot."[46]

Hit the spot he did, with sweeping curveballs, tempting

Pedro Martinez, pictured here at a 1999 press conference in Santo Domingo, Dominican Republic, holds up two fingers signifying being named a Cy Young Award winner for the second time in his career. Martinez, who became only the third player in major league history to win the award in both leagues, was 23-4 with a 2.07 ERA for the Red Sox in 1999.

change-ups, and well-placed fastballs. As Pedro's strikeouts mounted, Boston fans unveiled the K placards and waved the Dominican flag.

Meanwhile, Boston scored two runs in the first inning. The team tallied another two runs in the second inning. Roger Clemens left the game in the third after allowing a leadoff hit. Soon it was a rout, with Pedro posting the strikeouts, while his team supplied the hits. Pedro had eight Ks in the first four innings. Another in the fifth. In all, he pitched seven innings, allowing two Yankee hits and no runs, and striking out 12 batters, as Boston destroyed their rivals by a final score of 13-1.

Mighty Martinez had stopped the Yankee juggernaut and breathed new life into his team. He guaranteed at least two more games for the Red Sox—and if they could win, then Pedro would be ready for the deciding Game 7.

Unfortunately, as Yankee outfielder Paul O'Neill had groused about Pedro's 17-strikeout performance in September: "We didn't get beat by the Red Sox; we got beat by Pedro Martinez."[47] Without Pedro, the Red Sox were hapless. Boston pitcher Bret Saberhagen could not hold the Yankees the next day, and he lost the game to the New Yorkers by a final score of 9-2. The next day brought another loss to Boston, this time 6-1, and Boston fans could only be left wondering: if only they had *two* Pedros.

The Yankees went on to win the 1999 World Series over the Atlanta Braves, while Boston was left to nurse another loss, and another year—now 81 years and counting—without a World Series trophy.

Pedro finished the season with a 23-4 record, an ERA of 2.07, and an incredible 313 strikeouts. During the playoffs, he pitched 17 innings, giving up only three hits and no runs. A month later, Pedro was named the American League Cy Young Award winner. He thus became only the third pitcher up to that time—joining Gaylord Perry (who won in 1972 and 1978) and Randy Johnson (who won the National League Cy Young Award in 1999)—to win the award in both leagues.

Pitching coach Joe Kerrigan summed up Pedro's talent: "People just don't appreciate the command he has of the base-ball, the way he can manipulate the ball . . . he sinks it, rises it, cuts it. He's a magician, what can you say?"[48]

Times of Trial

When Pedro arrived in Florida for spring training in February 2000, he faced predictable questions: Could he possibly top what he had done in 1999? Would he win the Cy Young Award again?

Pedro was unperturbed. "Only God knows," he responded. "I'm not saying I can do it, and I'm not saying I can't. I don't have anything to prove. I'll just have to go do my job and see what happens."[49]

The Red Sox were facing their own questions: Could they unseat the Yankees this year? The New York team was aging—Roger Clemens was 37 years old—while Boston had the best pitcher in the league, backed up by brother Ramon and a couple of other good arms, along with shortstop Nomar Garciaparra and some other promising players.

The season opened on an upbeat note. Pedro went out to the mound in Seattle and struck out 11 batters in seven innings. The Red Sox beat the Mariners, 2-0.

Pedro went 5-0 in April. By the end of May, he had pitched a couple of shutouts, and even when he lost, he pitched well. On May 6, he came out on the wrong side of a game with the Tampa Bay Devil Rays. But he struck out 17 batters—matching his personal best against the Yankees that previous September—went seven scoreless innings, and only gave up one run. Unfortunately, the Red Sox couldn't get even one player across the plate, so Pedro lost the matchup, 1-0.

On May 28, the Red Sox faced the Yankees, with first place on the line. It was a rematch between Pedro Martinez and Roger Clemens—Cy Young versus Cy Old. When Pedro arrived at Yankee Stadium, he showed little sign of feeling pressure. "I like pitching here," he said matter-of-factly. "I like playing both here and Shea Stadium. It's in New York. A lot of Dominican people, loud fans, good competition, two good teams to beat."[50]

Both pitchers were in command that day. The game went into the ninth inning tied at 0-0. In the top of the ninth, Clemens got two men out. But then he misfielded a chopped grounder that came back to the mound and suddenly a Boston runner stood at first. Next up was right fielder Trot Nixon. He crushed a high Clemens fastball into the right-field stands. With one stroke of the bat, Boston burst ahead, 2-0.

Pedro came out for the ninth inning to finish the game. He hit the lead-off batter, sending him to first base. Then Yankee shortstop Derek Jeter rolled a single to right. The now-worried Red Sox were suddenly looking at two Yankees on base, no outs.

Pedro next faced Paul O'Neill and struck him out. Then Bernie Williams hit a high fly ball to right field. Pedro turned around to watch. A flurry of Yankees rushed out of the dugout to see if it was going over the fence for a home run. Right fielder Trot Nixon backed up to the wall. He reached up and caught the ball for the second out.

Incredibly, Martinez hit the next Yankee batter. The bases were now loaded, two outs, with the tying run on second base.

Yankee fans were standing, cheering, shouting. Pedro reared back and threw a fastball. The batter topped it and sent a slow grounder to second base. The throw to first was in time. The ballgame was over. Pedro won, 2-0. Boston climbed into first place.

The Red Sox went into June that year looking strong, but by the time the month was over, they were stumbling. The team had slipped to third place in the American League East, and Pedro was developing a sore shoulder. On June 30, he was placed on the disabled list. By that point, he had posted a record of 9-3, with a 1.44 ERA. Pedro thought he could still pitch, but Boston manager Jimy Williams wanted to protect his valuable arm.

Pedro stayed on the sidelines for two weeks. He was picked for the All-Star team for the fifth year in a row, but he sat out the game because of his shoulder. He came back on July 13, 2000, and pitched seven strong innings against the Mets, as the Red Sox went on to beat the "other" New York team, 4-3. A few days later, Pedro struck out 12 to beat his old team, the Montreal Expos, 3-1.

Then, on July 23, in Fenway Park, he gave another one of his masterpiece performances. He went up against the Chicago White Sox and pitched nine innings—throwing a total of 131 pitches. He struck out 15 White Sox, yielded no walks, and no runs, as the Red Sox took the game, 1-0. "That's as good as it gets, pitching-wise," said manager Jimy Williams. "I didn't manage this game, I watched it, same as you did." Not for the first time, Pedro's manager beamed with pride: "I hope people appreciate what they saw today."[51]

During the game, the White Sox complained that the plate umpire made the strike zone too big. Pedro later admitted that was probably true—he, too, had noticed the umpire was giving the pitchers an extra inch or two on the outside of the plate. "I analyze every umpire," Martinez explained. "Right away I saw that." So he took advantage of the situation, throwing plenty of outside pitches. "You have to be smart," Pedro continued. "If you have the experience, you use it."[52]

The Chicago manager was ejected from the game for arguing about the larger-than-normal strike zone. Then a Chicago coach was thrown out when he waved a towel at the umpire, suggesting he was making the strike zone as big as the towel. Pedro commented: "If they give me a plate the size of a towel? I guarantee I'll strike out 20 of them."[53]

Later, the ousted Chicago manager admitted, "He's one of the premier pitchers in the game, no question about it."[54]

He was right. No question Pedro was a top pitcher—and no question that Pedro was used to controversy and not intimidated by it.

There were two occasions in 2000 when Pedro's pitching style brought about bench-clearing incidents. On April 30, Pedro faced the Cleveland Indians—the same team he had knocked out of the playoffs the previous October. In the third inning, Cleveland catcher Einar Diaz hit a double off Martinez. In the fifth, Diaz smacked another double. When the Cleveland catcher came up again in the seventh, Pedro threw a high, inside pitch. Then he threw another, even closer. Diaz spun away and fell to the ground.

An angry buzz emerged from the Cleveland dugout—the Indians thought maybe Pedro was throwing at Diaz in retaliation for the two hits. But nothing happened. Pedro ended up striking out Diaz and left the Indians scoreless for the inning.

The Red Sox came up to bat in the eighth. Second baseman Jose Offerman led off the inning for Boston. On his first pitch, the Cleveland pitcher hit Offerman on the leg. Players from each team rushed onto the field. There were angry words, and some shoving and wrestling, as Boston players accused the Cleveland pitcher of throwing at Offerman on purpose. But no punches were thrown. The umpires restored order.

The Indians came to bat in the bottom of the inning. Cleveland second baseman Roberto Alomar stepped up. Pedro threw an inside pitch that hit Alomar below the hip. Again, players rushed onto the field. This time the Indians were accusing Pedro of throwing at Alomar on purpose. After order was restored, the umpires ejected both Martinez and manager Jimy Williams from the game.

"Robbie Alomar is the last person I want to hit," Pedro insisted later. "But it's part of the game. Those things happen. Baseball has been like this forever."[55]

The Red Sox won the game, 2-1, and this latest victory made Martinez 7-0 against the Indians—including postseason games—since he had come to the American League. Martinez, however, did receive a five-game suspension, along with an undisclosed fine, as punishment for his alleged indiscretion— although Pedro stood by his denial that he purposely tried to hit anybody.

Later in that same season, at the end of August, another incident occurred in Tampa, Florida. By this time the Red Sox were struggling, but still hoping to claw their way into the wild-card spot. Boston had lost to the Tampa Devil Rays on August 28. Pedro was pitching the next day. The first batter for the Devil Rays was Gerald Williams.

With a count of one ball and two strikes, Pedro threw a 95-mile-an-hour fastball on the inside part of the plate. The ball spun off toward Williams and hit him on the left forearm. Williams hesitated for a moment, rubbing his arm, before taking his base. He started walking toward first base, then veered off and charged the pitcher's mound, shoving Pedro back and taking a swing at him. "He pushed me back," reported Pedro, "and then as he was falling down, he threw a punch at me, and got me on the arms, but he really didn't hit me."[56]

The Boston players ran out to protect Pedro. Tampa team members rushed to join the fray. When the brawl was over, Gerald Williams was ejected from the game, as was the Devil Rays' manager. Several players emerged from the pile rubbing their arms, dusting themselves off.

But Pedro—he just went back to pitching.

In the third inning, the Devil Rays' starting pitcher hit Boston first baseman Brian Daubach and then shortstop

During the 2000 season, Pedro Martinez got into an altercation with Tampa Bay Devil Rays outfielder Gerald Williams after Martinez hit Williams with a fastball. Martinez kept his composure and went on to record the third one-hitter of his career, an 8-0 win in which he struck out 13 Devil Rays batters.

Nomar Garciaparra. The Devil Rays' pitcher was ejected from the game.

Pedro just kept pitching.

In the seventh inning, the Devil Rays' reliever threw a pitch at Daubach. There was another brawl on the mound; yet another Devil Rays pitcher got the boot.

Pedro just kept pitching—until he came out to start the ninth inning and the fans cheered as they realized not one Tampa player had a hit. Amid all the disruption, Pedro was quietly working on a no-hitter.

In the ninth inning, the Devil Rays' catcher flicked a single to right field to break up Pedro's no-hitter. But the Red Sox won, 8-0, and Pedro struck out 13 on the way to chalking up the third one-hitter of his career.

Eight Devil Rays had been ejected from the game. Four batters had been hit—the one Devil Ray and three Red Sox—but Pedro kept his composure and did his job. "I just wanted to remain calm and do the things I have to do to win the game," said Pedro. "I thought it was more important than plunking somebody. As close as we are [in the playoff race], I thought it was more important to win this game. I can't afford to get thrown out and get suspended. I need to help my team down the stretch."[57]

Boston manager Jimy Williams backed up Pedro that night. "Teams can try to rattle him, but things don't bother him. He keeps them in perspective. Someone has to be in control of his mental faculties out there, and he is. You factor in his stuff and that's what puts him in that upper echelon of pitchers. That's how great this kid is."[58]

Pedro finished the 2000 season 18-6, with four shutouts. He led the American League in strikeouts with 284. He also led the league with a 1.74 ERA—almost two runs better than the 3.70 ERA of the second-place finisher, who just happened to be Pedro's rival, Roger Clemens.

Clemens did go on to postseason play with the New York Yankees (which beat their crosstown rivals, the New York Mets, for the World Series title), while Pedro's Red Sox sputtered to a second-place finish in their division, six games out of the wild-card spot. But Pedro again won the Cy Young Award—a unanimous selection for the second year in a row—and became just the seventh pitcher in history to win the award three times.

As good as the season was for Pedro, though, it was just as challenging for his brother Ramon, who struggled through 2000 with a 10-8 record and a miserable 6.13 ERA. At the end of the season, Ramon left Boston and his brother to go back to the Los Angeles Dodgers—but they ended up not needing him, and so, at age 33, he signed with the Pittsburgh Pirates. His arm didn't feel well in 2001. He started out the season with the Pirates but was not in top form, posting an 0-2 record. In May 2001, Ramon retired from baseball and went back to the Dominican Republic.

SEASONS OUT OF THE SUN

For the Red Sox, the 2001 season was a carbon copy of the 2000 season. The team started out strong, and Boston was in first place in June. But the Red Sox struggled down the stretch, finishing worse than in 2000—$13^1/_2$ games behind the Yankees in the American League East.

Pedro, too, started out strong. By the end of May, he was 7-1, with a 1.44 ERA. In June, though, Pedro began to feel a strain in his right shoulder. It got sore and swelled up after he pitched. He nursed it along, went for tests, missed a couple of starts. Finally, at the end of June, Pedro went on the disabled list with right-shoulder tendonitis.

All of Red Sox Nation hoped it was nothing worse. Pedro was in his ninth full season in the majors. His brother Ramon had been in *his* ninth season when he tore the rotator cuff in his right shoulder and had to go for reconstructive surgery—and Ramon was never the same afterwards.

Pedro had tests in Massachusetts that showed an inflammation around his right rotator cuff—but nothing worse. He went to California for a second opinion and got the same diagnosis. Unlike his brother, Pedro would not need an operation, and he flew home to the Dominican Republic to rest up.

Pedro was back in Boston later in July and taking practice in the bullpen in August, as the Red Sox dropped in the standings. When Pedro left, the Red Sox were ahead of the Yankees by three games. By mid-August they were four games behind. "I'm not used to sitting down," said Pedro. "It's been uncomfortable. If we're going to struggle, we should struggle all together, not just me sitting at home and watching TV and getting desperate, not being able to do anything."[59]

Meanwhile, with the team faltering, Red Sox manager Jimy

Williams lost his job, succeeded by pitching coach Joe Kerrigan. Under Kerrigan, Pedro made his first comeback effort on August 26. He threw four innings and struck out four batters, but the Red Sox lost the game, 5-4. A week later Pedro pitched again, against the Yankees, and lasted six innings, allowing no runs. But again, Boston went on to lose, this time 2-1.

With the Red Sox sinking fast, Pedro made the decision to play it safe and rest his arm. He only pitched a few more innings, ending the year with a meager 7-3 record. Still, he posted a 2.39 ERA for his shortened season and struck out 163 batters in 116 innings. Not bad for someone with an aching shoulder.

That year, after September 11, 2001, Red Sox fans found themselves in the unfamiliar position of rooting for the Yankees to bring the World Championship back to terror-ravaged New York City. The Yankees almost did but fell short—beating the Seattle Mariners for the ALCS but losing 4 games to 3 to the Arizona Diamondbacks in the World Series. Pedro was not in the running for the Cy Young Award that year. Instead, it went to the former Red Sox pitcher and current Pedro rival, Yankee pitching ace Roger Clemens.

In December, the Red Sox were sold to a new ownership group. "We'll give the Yankees a real run for their money starting next year," predicted John Henry, the billionaire money manager who headed the group that bought the Red Sox. One of his partners scoffed, "The curse of the Bambino? We prefer to think of it as a spell we intend to break."[60]

General Manager Dan Duquette—the man who brought Pedro Martinez to Boston—was sent packing, as was new manager Joe Kerrigan. In March 2002, the owners picked Grady Little as the next Red Sox manager. Little had managed in the minor leagues for 16 seasons, before moving up to coach in the majors in Boston and Cleveland.

Meanwhile, Pedro went home to the Dominican Republic to rehabilitate his shoulder, taking on a careful strength and conditioning program. His regimen was designed to increase

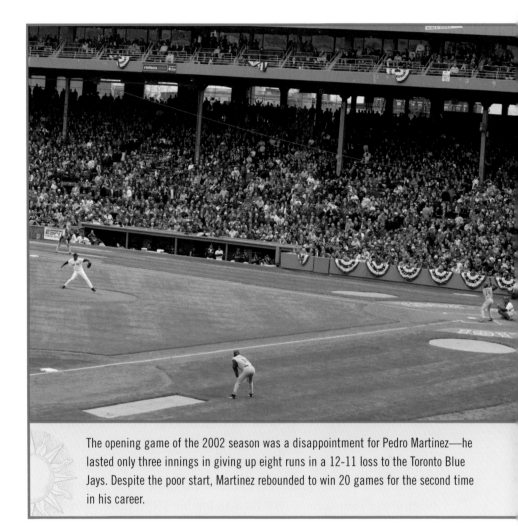

The opening game of the 2002 season was a disappointment for Pedro Martinez—he lasted only three innings in giving up eight runs in a 12-11 loss to the Toronto Blue Jays. Despite the poor start, Martinez rebounded to win 20 games for the second time in his career.

his upper-body strength, especially around the shoulders. When Pedro arrived in Fort Myers, Florida, for spring training, he was 15 pounds heavier than the previous season, feeling strong and ready to go. "My arm feels really great," he reported. But he also cautioned: "I can't go 137 or 127 pitches like I used to. I have to be careful about that. If I have to stay an inning less than I used to I'll have to do that. I don't want my career to end yet. I have to be cautious."[61]

Still, who would complain if Pedro no longer felt comfortable pitching a complete nine-inning game? Hardly any pitchers did that anymore. If Pedro could throw a strong seven innings—which for him involved an average of about a hundred pitches—he still could be the best pitcher in the game.

Pedro took the mound on opening day 2002, against the Toronto Blue Jays, and gave up a worrisome eight runs in the three innings he pitched (Toronto eventually won, 12-11). But Pedro soon righted himself, beating the Baltimore Orioles the following week, and taking on the Yankees a few days after that, as the Red Sox won by a score of 7-6. Soon Pedro was pitching shutouts again, breezing by the Kansas City Royals, 4-0, and the Baltimore Orioles, 7-0, on his way to yet another winning season.

Boston beat New York in five out of their first six matchups, and in May led the American League East division. But, true to form—and despite Pedro's best efforts—the Red Sox faltered, letting the Yankees pull ahead in the standings.

The Red Sox sent seven players to the All-Star Game—including Pedro, who had missed the previous year—but still could not mount a serious challenge to New York. The 2002 season, once again, saw the Red Sox settling for second place, and like the previous two seasons, unable to earn a wild-card berth.

During the late stages of the season, Pedro took some time off due to a pulled groin muscle. But he came back strong, beating the Tampa Bay Devil Rays to log his 150th career win. He finished with a 20-4 record, the second 20-win season of his career. He led the league in both ERA (2.26) and strikeouts (239), but he came in second in the Cy Young vote to Barry Zito of the Oakland Athletics. Fellow Boston pitcher Derek Lowe followed Pedro by taking third place.

Pedro tried to be philosophical about the season, and watching the Yankees march off to postseason play, he downplayed the competition between the two clubs. "There's no rivalry," said Martinez. "I love Bernie Williams. I love Derek Jeter. I love everybody. We just compete. We're not part of that Babe Ruth stuff. We don't have anything to do with it. I wasn't even born then."[62]

When asked about the Red Sox long dry spell in the World Series, Pedro merely responded, "I believe in God. I don't believe in curses."[63]

Perhaps. But soon Martinez would be back in the thick of things, embroiled in that long rivalry with the team from New York—even more than he ever was before and more than he could ever know.

6

Oh, So Close!

The first week of the 2003 Red Sox season might have foretold the tale for the rest of the year. Pedro started the opener against the Tampa Bay Devil Rays. He pitched a strong seven innings, striking out six batters and allowing three hits, before leaving the game with Boston ahead, 4-1. But Boston blew the lead, as the Devil Rays rallied for five runs in the ninth inning and took the game, 6-4.

A few days later, Martinez went up against the Baltimore Orioles. This time he lasted eight innings, allowing four hits and one run. In the bottom of the ninth, however, with the game tied at 1-1, the Orioles loaded the bases. Then Boston's reliever walked in the go-ahead run.

"There's not much I can do after I give you seven or eight innings," said Pedro, who after two games boasted an ERA of only 0.70 but had yet to post a win. "You just have to hope that someone

One of Boston's key free-agent acquisitions during the 2003 off-season was designated hitter/first baseman David Ortiz. The Dominican slugger posted career bests in home runs (31), RBI (101), and slugging percentage (.592) in helping to lead the Red Sox back into the playoffs for the first time since 1999.

comes in after you and does the job. You just pray to God that they do the job."[64]

Yet, for all their foibles, the Red Sox managed to progress through the season, winning more than they lost—thanks to Pedro on the mound and some strong hitting by shortstop Nomar Garciaparra, outfielders Johnny Damon and Trot Nixon, and two other players Pedro helped bring to the team—both of them Dominicans. Outfielder Manny Ramirez had come to Boston in 2001 from the Cleveland Indians, after Pedro told the slugger that Boston would be a great place for him to play. Then in 2003, Pedro sang the praises of Boston to David Ortiz, another slugger, who joined the Red Sox after six years with the Minnesota Twins.

Some more good news came early in the 2003 season. The Red Sox decided to exercise their option for the extra year in Pedro's contract. So Martinez would remain with the team not only for 2003 but for 2004 as well. What would happen after that, no one knew.

Over the Fourth of July weekend, 2003, Boston fans traveled to Yankee Stadium for a four-game series. In the first game, Red Sox hitters drilled seven home runs to beat the Yankees, 10-3.

FENWAY'S DOMINICAN MAFIA

Nearly 400 baseball players from the Dominican Republic have made it to the major leagues, going back to the days of Juan Marichal and Felipe Alou. During the 2003 and 2004 seasons, three very special men played together on the Red Sox, forming a kind of Dominican Mafia.

First and foremost was Pedro Martinez, the slender pitching ace who joined the team in 1998. Then there was the dread-locked Manny Ramirez, who has been called the best hitter on the planet. Pedro had talked to Manny a number of times and convinced him that Boston was a great place to play. So in 2001, the outfielder made the move to the Red Sox.

A year younger than Pedro, Manny was born in Santo Domingo, but his family moved to New York City when he was a child and he grew up in the shadow of Yankee Stadium. He played eight years for the Cleveland Indians as a right fielder, then switched over to left field when he joined the Red Sox. He has consistently batted over .300 and hit with power—37 home runs in 2003 and 43 in 2004.

Rounding out the trio was slugger David Ortiz, who fans

In the second game, Yankee pitcher Roger Clemens threw a fastball that hit Boston infielder Kevin Millar in the hand. Millar took his base. The Boston trainer checked over Millar at first base, as Red Sox players glared at Clemens, suspecting he had done it on purpose. Then Boston outfielder Trot Nixon stepped to the plate. He swung at the first pitch and launched a home run into right-center field. That was the Boston answer to Clemens. The Red Sox won, 10-2, and at that point they were only two games out of first place.

The next day, Yankee pitcher Andy Pettitte quieted the Red Sox, and the Yankees took the game, 7-1. The last game

called "Big Papi" or "Señor Papi." Pedro talked to him as well, and soon Big Papi, too, was headed for Boston. The youngest of the group, he was born in Santo Domingo in 1975. A big guy, at six foot four and 230 pounds, he played six years for the Minnesota Twins before joining the Red Sox in 2003. Big Papi batted .288 with 31 home runs in 2003, and for the championship season improved his batting average to .301, with 41 home runs.

In 2004, Ramirez and Ortiz formed a powerful duo in the Boston lineup—Ramirez typically batted third and Ortiz followed in the cleanup position. They each hit more than 40 home runs, sported a batting average over .300, and posted more than 100 RBI. The last pair to accomplish this feat was Lou Gehrig and Babe Ruth when they played together for the Yankees in 1931. Ramirez and Ortiz also hit back-to-back home runs six times during the 2004 season, tying a major league record.

After the 2004 season, Ramirez and Ortiz remained in Boston. Pedro went on to join another Dominican Mafia.

of the series brought Yankee pitcher Mike Mussina face-to-face with Pedro Martinez.

The Red Sox scored a run in the first inning. Pedro took the mound in the bottom of the first and hit the leadoff batter, second baseman Alfonso Soriano, in the hand with an inside fastball. Then Derek Jeter stepped up. Pedro threw another ball inside and the pitch hit Jeter.

Both Soriano and Jeter went to the hospital for X rays, which were negative. The players were OK. But did Martinez hit them in retaliation for the game on Saturday, when Clemens had hit Millar?

That's what Yankee manager Joe Torre suspected. Yankee third-base coach Willie Randolph was more direct: "I was fuming . . . I thought 'They're trying to take my guys out.' I was steamed. I just wanted to get somebody."[65] Owner George Steinbrenner thundered: "If he threw at them to try and deliver a message, he delivered the wrong [expletive] message! The first two hitters? Are you kidding?"[66]

But Pedro denied it. "The only way you're going to get Soriano out is inside," he insisted. "When you throw inside, you're going to hit guys sometimes. I don't try to hit anybody, it was just an accident."[67] He also pointed out the pitch to Jeter wasn't even a fastball. Presumably, Jeter could have gotten out of the way if he'd tried. "The guys are on top of the plate," Pedro said. "Jeter's was a sinker. He just went into it."[68] Later, both Soriano and Jeter said they were not angry at Martinez.

The Red Sox held their lead as Martinez pitched six scoreless innings. In the seventh, Pedro let in one run to tie the game. Pedro left at the end of the inning, having struck out 11 Yankees. Then, in the ninth, two Yankee hits plus a Boston error brought in a run for New York, and the game ended 2-1 for the Yankees. "If there's a blueprint for beating Pedro, that's the blueprint. Keep it close and hope for a break," said Yankee manager Joe Torre. "He doesn't give you much."[69]

The Red Sox had made a move, winning the first two

games, but they lost the next two and ended up right where they started: four games behind in the standings.

By September, the Red Sox and Yankees had battled back and forth several times—and they were in the same position. The Red Sox then went to New York. Pedro was on the mound, and he took charge, striking out nine Yankees in six innings. The Red Sox won the game, 9-3. A day later the Red Sox bombed the Yankees in an 11-0 blowout, and suddenly the Red Sox were only $1^1/_2$ games behind the league leaders.

The Red Sox kept up their winning ways. Pedro threw a 5-0 shutout against Baltimore, then pitched a 2-0 shutout against Cleveland. A few days later, the Red Sox clinched a playoff berth with a lopsided 14-3 win over the Orioles.

The Yankees did not falter and retained their first-place position. For the first time in three years, though, the Red Sox were headed for postseason play. Pedro would not win the coveted Cy Young Award—his 14-4 won-lost record was bested by several American League pitchers—but he did come in second in the American League for strikeouts, with 206, and once again posted the lowest ERA in the league.

CONFLICTS AND CONFRONTATIONS

If it weren't for all that happened later, the ALDS between the Boston Red Sox and the Oakland A's would have been one for the history books. In the first game, Pedro gave up three runs in the third inning. He went into the seventh with a 4-3 lead, and allowed a hit and two walks. The bases were loaded. But Pedro, always a cool customer, got the last Oakland batter to hit a weak pop-up to end the inning.

Pedro wore out his arm throwing 130 pitches that day— some 30 pitches over his self-imposed limit—and in the end it was all for naught. Pedro left the game with a 4-3 lead, but Oakland scored a run in the ninth to send the matchup into extra innings. In the twelfth inning, the A's loaded the bases, then a surprise bunt brought in the winning run from third.

In Game 2 of the playoffs, the Red Sox went up against

Pedro Martinez walks off the field after Boston's 4-3, Game 5 win over the Oakland Athletics in the 2003 American League Division Series. Martinez pitched seven innings and gave up seven hits and three runs in the victory.

Barry Zito, the Oakland ace who had won the Cy Young Award the year before. The outcome was never in doubt: Boston lost, 5-1. The Red Sox now found themselves in a familiar place:

They were down 2-0, facing elimination in the best-of-five series.

Back in Boston for Game 3, the Red Sox and A's were tied 1-1 after nine innings, then Trot Nixon banged a home run in the eleventh inning to win the game. The next day, an eighth-inning double gave the Red Sox a 5-4 victory over the A's. Now the series was tied at 2-2.

The deciding Game 5 pitted Oakland's Cy Young Award winner, Barry Zito, against Boston's Cy Young Award winner, Pedro Martinez. Pedro pitched seven innings and again—like the first game of the series—left the mound with his team ahead, 4-3. This time, however, the Red Sox were able to hold on for the win. They took three games in a row for a startling comeback, and the chance to face the Yankees once again.

The only problem: Pedro had just pitched. He would not be ready again until Game 3 of the ALCS.

There would be two games in New York, three in Boston, and if necessary another two in New York. The Red Sox took the first game at Yankee Stadium, 5-2, behind pitcher Tim Wakefield. In Game 2, it was the Yankees' turn. The pinstripes posted a 6-2 victory.

Red Sox Nation felt comfortable with a tie as the series moved north to New England. Boston would have home-field advantage for the next three games—and the energy and passion of Red Sox fans made home-field advantage worth something!

Also, Pedro was pitching—not once, but twice, if the Red Sox needed him. Game 3 featured another rematch between Pedro Martinez and Roger Clemens, whose rivalry had begun when it was Cy Young versus Cy Old back in 1999. This time, October 11, 2003, the Red Sox took an early lead with two runs in the first inning.

In the second, Jorge Posada stroked a double off Pedro. Then Yankee outfielder Karim Garcia sliced a curveball into right field, to bring in a run. The next inning, Derek Jeter tied the game at 2-2, when he tagged a Martinez curveball for a home run.

In the fourth, Martinez gave up a walk to Posada, plus two hits, to allow another Yankee run. Then right fielder Karim Garcia came up again. On the first pitch, Pedro hurled a brushback fastball that got away from him and sailed behind Garcia's head. The ball careened off Garcia. On the video replay, it showed the pitch actually seemed to hit off Garcia's bat—or was it his shoulder? The umpire ruled the pitch hit Garcia.

The Yankee batter clearly thought Pedro had thrown at him on purpose. He yelled at Martinez. Several Yankees also shouted at Martinez from the dugout—including the aging Yankee coach Don Zimmer, who once had also served as manager of the Red Sox back in the 1970s.

But whatever the call, Garcia was now on first, and the bases were loaded.

Yankee Alfonso Soriano stepped up and bounced a ground ball to second base. Karim Garcia slid hard into second to try to break up the double play—and maybe rough up the Boston second baseman in return for getting the Pedro brushback.

Boston made the double play as another run scored. The inning then ended on a pop-out—but not the yelling. Pedro and Karim Garcia shouted at each other. Jorge Posada screamed out at Martinez. Pedro responded by yelling back at Posada, then pointing to his head and pointing toward the dugout. Did Pedro mean that he would hit Posada in the head?

The umpires warned both teams—but the umpires were talking to some pretty tough customers. Roger Clemens came to the mound, with a 4-2 lead, and faced Boston outfielder Manny Ramirez. Clemens immediately got aggressive, and on the 1-2 pitch threw a high, inside fastball. Ramirez shouted and cursed at Clemens and started walking toward the mound, baseball bat in hand. The two teams rushed to defend their teammates, meeting for a wrestling match halfway between home plate and the pitcher's mound.

Pedro tried to stay out of the fray, standing behind first base. But suddenly Yankee coach Don Zimmer, 72 years old, came charging after him. Zimmer's hand was raised toward Martinez as he rushed the pitcher. Pedro sidestepped the lunging Zimmer, pushed him on the back of the neck, and Zimmer went down, rolling onto the ground. The aging Yankee coach was clearly dazed, bleeding from the bridge of his nose, and he didn't get up right away. The old man's fall shocked the players and stopped the fight.

After Zimmer was helped off the field, and the players and the coaches calmed down, the game resumed. No one was ejected, and Zimmer watched the rest of the game from the bench, with a Band-Aid prominently displayed on his nose.

Manny Ramirez ended his turn at bat by striking out. Clemens got more revenge in the sixth inning, just before he retired from the game, by getting Ramirez to hit into a double play to end the inning.

Pedro did not allow any more runs. But the damage was done. The Red Sox went down in this controversial game, 4-3, to fall behind in the series, 2-1.

At the end of the game there was another dustup, as Karim Garcia and a fellow Yankee got in a shoving match with a Boston groundskeeper, who, they claimed, was waving a towel and cheering for the Red Sox. It was a messy end to a messy game, one that caused both embarrassment and concern among many in baseball circles. Said Red Sox manager Grady Little, "When this series began everyone knew it was going to be quite a battle, very emotional, with a lot of intensity, but I think we've upgraded it from a battle to a war."[70]

Fortunately, the next day, a Sunday, it rained and there was no game, allowing frayed nerves to settle. Meanwhile, a tearful Don Zimmer apologized for his actions at a press conference and stated that he did not blame Pedro.

Pedro himself insisted he had not intended to hit Karim

Garcia. "I didn't throw at him on purpose."[71] Pedro's manager, as well as his teammates, stood behind him. "Pedro never takes a shot at someone's head like that or up in that area," said manager Grady Little. "But in their opinion, it was, so there you go."[72]

As for the incident behind first base, Pedro commented that he was shocked at the sight of Zimmer coming his way, and yes, he did believe that Zimmer intended to slug him. That explains why he pushed him to the ground. "But I wouldn't have hit him," Martinez said. "I could never do it."[73]

The incident quickly made the national news, actually overshadowing the outcome of the game. It was soon even the subject of parodies on TV shows like *Saturday Night Live*.

In the end, baseball authorities fined Martinez $50,000. They also clipped Manny Ramirez for $25,000, and Karim Garcia for $10,000. Don Zimmer had to forfeit $5,000 for his run at Pedro.

The Yankee victory in Fenway Park also gave them a 2-1 lead in the series, and if fate had anything to say about it, there could very well be a final game replay of a Pedro Martinez versus Roger Clemens showdown.

GAME 7

Indeed, the fates did intervene. The Red Sox went on to win Game 4 behind Tim Wakefield, to tie the series, 2-2. Then the Yankees won Game 5.

The two teams traveled to New York, with Boston's back against the wall. The Red Sox had to take both games in Yankee Stadium to win the series. In Game 6, the Red Sox survived a scare, falling behind 6-4 by the seventh inning, then rallying for three runs and getting two more in the ninth on a Trot Nixon homer, winning the day, 9-6.

"I guess it was supposed to come down to seven games," said Yankee manager Joe Torre. "I don't know of any two clubs that are more evenly matched than we are."[74]

Boston's Kevin Millar said it another way: "The gods of baseball wanted to see this happen."[75]

The day, October 16, 2003, brought a sellout crowd to Yankee Stadium. Pedro was protected by police as he warmed up in the bullpen before the game.

The game started out in Boston's favor. Pedro was cruising. In the second inning, the Red Sox scored three runs on a Trot Nixon home run and a Yankee error. Red Sox first baseman Kevin Millar led off the fourth with a solo home run, and Boston's lead increased to 4-0. Later in the same inning, with Boston men on first and third, Yankee manager Joe Torre came out to the mound to take out Roger Clemens. The Rocket was gone.

Torre brought in one of his stars, Mike Mussina, to relieve Clemens, and Mussina got the Red Sox out on a double play. Then the Yankees came up in the fifth, and Jason Giambi led off with a home run. So what? Now it was 4-1. Pedro looked strong. It was only a matter of time.

After Giambi, Pedro put away the rest of the Yankees in the fifth, and he cut through Yankee batters in the sixth as well. It was still 4-1, Boston.

As the fateful Yankee pinch-hitter Aaron Boone later recalled, "It's Game 7; it's Pedro; we're down, there's no chance. It ain't looking good. We were going to have to scratch and claw."[76]

In the bottom of the seventh, Jason Giambi stroked another solo home run. But in the top of the eighth, Boston's David Ortiz responded with a home run of his own. The score stood at 5-2. Only six more outs to go.

Red Sox fans thought that Pedro was now done for the day. He had pitched his seven innings, allowing three hits—two of them Giambi home runs. At the end of the seventh, Pedro had given a little kiss and pointed up to the sky—his usual sign that he'd finished his job. When he walked into the dugout, several Boston players went over to congratulate him

Pedro Martinez walks toward the Boston dugout after being pulled from Game 7 of the 2003 American League Championship Series. Martinez pitched 7 1/3 innings, allowing five earned runs in the 11-inning, 6-5 loss to the New York Yankees.

on his fine performance. They gave him a hug, raised their hands in high fives. "I always want to stay in the game," Pedro later said. "But I thought I was coming out."[77]

Instead, in the bottom of the eighth, Pedro walked back out to the mound. The fans were puzzled. He had said good-bye. He'd pitched his seven innings, thrown his hundred pitches. What was he doing?

Pedro got the first Yankee batter to pop up for an out. Then he faced Derek Jeter, and got ahead with two strikes. Pedro threw the next ball over the plate, and Jeter lined it to right field for a double.

By now Pedro had thrown 110 pitches, and he was clearly getting tired. The fans knew it, as they shouted for the benefit of the Red Sox manager: "Get him out!"

Up stepped Bernie Williams, who punched a ground ball up the middle for a single. Jeter scored. It was 5-3.

Manager Grady Little finally came out of the dugout and walked to the mound. He talked with Pedro. Instead of calling for a reliever, though, he patted his pitcher on the shoulder and returned to the dugout. Red Sox fans were screaming. What was wrong with Grady Little? Why didn't he yank the faltering Boston ace?

The next Yankee batter was Hideki Matsui. Pedro got two strikes on the left-handed hitter. Then he threw a fastball. But Pedro was tired. The fastball wasn't that fast. Matsui pulled the ball down the right-field line for a ground-rule double. Now Bernie Williams was on third base. And Matsui, the tying run, stood on second—with one out.

Grady Little didn't move. There were sinking stomachs in the stands, in all of Red Sox Nation. Yankee catcher Jorge Posada came up and watched two balls and a strike. Then he swung and missed. The count was 2-2.

Pedro threw a fastball. Posada got a piece of it and lofted a fly ball to shallow center field. The Boston shortstop went out. The second baseman went out. The center fielder came in. The ball dropped right in the middle of all three of them.

Williams scored. Matsui scored. The game was now tied at 5-5. Grady Little walked out to the mound again, and this time he finally took out Pedro, calling for a reliever who got the last two outs of the inning.

The Red Sox came up in the ninth, the game tied at 5-5. They were in shock at their sudden reversal of fortune and went scoreless in the inning. But so did the Yankees in the bottom of the ninth.

The game went into extra innings. The tenth was scoreless. The Red Sox failed to score in the top of the eleventh.

The Yankees came up. Pinch-hitter Aaron Boone led off, facing Boston's Tim Wakefield. "I considered taking a pitch," Boone later said, "but then I said, 'Ah, just get a good one and go after it.' I finally put a good swing on one. I guess it was my time."[78] Boone swung on the first pitch. It was a high fly ball to left field. Boone said he knew right away it was a home run.

Once again the Boston Red Sox fell to their arch rivals. Considering how close they came to winning—a mere six outs—it was perhaps the most agonizing defeat of them all.

The Yankees went on to lose to the Florida Marlins in the 2003 World Series. But the ultimate Yankee fate did not matter to Red Sox Nation. Fans and critics alike blamed manager Grady Little for the latest Red Sox humiliation—for failing to recognize that Pedro was getting tired, for lacking the courage to go to his bullpen, for freezing at the crucial moment of decision.

Grady Little, in his own defense, said, "Pedro Martinez had been our man all year long and in situations like that, he's the one we want on the mound over anybody else we can bring in out of that bullpen."[79]

Pedro himself tried to take the blame: "I am the ace of the team. You have to trust me. There's no time to say I'm tired. There's no reason to blame Grady. I was the one pitching. I was the one who gave up the lead. I was responsible for the pitches I made."[80] Pedro told the fans: "If anyone wants to point a finger, point it at me."[81]

Within days, however, Grady Little was gone from Boston. As for Pedro, he would be around to fight another day, another year—one more chance to reverse the Curse.

7

Why Not Us?

During the off-season, Boston signed another starting pitcher to bolster the ranks—Curt Schilling, a power thrower who had played nine seasons with the Philadelphia Phillies and then gone on to help the Arizona Diamondbacks win the World Series in 2001. The Red Sox also signed a reliever, Keith Foulke, from the Oakland A's, as well as infielder Pokey Reese from the Pittsburgh Pirates.

But the most significant change was in the manager's seat. Grady Little was out. Terry Francona was in.

Francona had been manager of the Philadelphia Phillies from 1997 through 2000, when Curt Schilling was on the team. One problem: As manager, Francona never had a winning season. He then spent a couple of years as a coach in Texas and Oakland, but even with that extra experience, he did not inspire great hope in Red Sox Nation.

It had become almost automatic that Pedro Martinez would pitch the season opener for the Red Sox, and this new year of 2004

On December 4, 2003, Terry Francona was named the 44th manager in Boston franchise history. Although Francona was only 285-363 in four years (1997–2000) as manager of the Philadelphia Phillies, Red Sox President Larry Lucchino (left) and General Manager Theo Epstein (right) had confidence in Francona's managerial skills.

was no different. Pedro took the mound on April 4. It was a cold night in Baltimore—the temperature was 43 degrees and dipped into the 30s as the evening progressed.

Pedro grew up in the heat of the Dominican Republic. He likes to pitch in Pedro weather—hazy, hot, and humid. This was not Pedro weather—and it was not Pedro's night.

In the first, Pedro gave up a couple of hits, and only got out of the inning with no damage because outfielder Manny Ramirez rocketed a throw to newcomer Pokey Reese and got a Baltimore runner out at third base. In the second inning, things got worse—real fast. Pedro's first pitch was a high fastball, cracked into the left-field seats for a home run. Then Pedro hit batter David Segui in the back. When the next batter rolled a grounder back to Pedro, he picked it up and tossed it to first base—only Pedro's throw was wide and skidded off the end of first baseman Kevin Millar's glove. A Baltimore run came in. The next batter poked a single, bringing in a third run.

Some observers wondered if Pedro was having trouble gripping the ball in the cold weather. Whatever the problem, Pedro finally settled down. He struck out the next two batters and got the third out on a long fly ball.

Pedro was out of the inning—finally. He then pitched through another four innings without giving up a run, but Boston batters failed to bail him out. The Red Sox went down in their season opener.

Pedro left the ballpark in frustration that night, before the game was even over, causing critics to question his support of the team. Pedro said he was only mad at himself, and Terry Francona insisted there was no problem with his star pitcher. "He had a tough second inning," said the new manager. "Other than that, he was very, very good."[82]

"Nothing went right for us. We just weren't good," summed up Boston outfielder Johnny Damon, who did not get a hit in his fives at-bats. "There are going to be better days."[83]

Better days there were, although Pedro's season—just like the entire Red Sox saga—remained uneven and dramatically unpredictable, right to the end. In his next outing, against the Toronto Blue Jays, Pedro faced 2003 American League Cy Young Award winner Roy Halladay. The first five innings provided a tough pitcher's duel, with no runs, only a scattering of base runners, and lots of Ks. In the bottom of the sixth, David Ortiz came up with a man on base—and cracked a ball into right field that kept going and going, until it hit the roof of the bullpen. Boston was ahead, 2-0.

Later, Pedro gave up a solo homer, but the Red Sox took the game, 4-1. Chalk up Pedro's first win of the season. Boston was on its way.

The Yankees came to Fenway Park in April, and Boston took three out of four games. The next weekend, Boston went to Yankee Stadium for a three-game series. Boston won the first matchup in a breeze, 11-2, and the second one in extra innings, when Manny Ramirez doubled and came home on a long fly ball to center field.

The next day, April 25, Pedro took the mound for the sweep amidst a chorus of boos from Yankee fans. No matter. In the first inning, Pedro struck out leadoff hitter Derek Jeter. Then he got Bernie Williams to ground out. And Alex Rodriguez—A-Rod—was put out by Boston first baseman Kevin Millar.

In the top of the fourth, Manny Ramirez stepped to the plate with a man on first base. The count went to two strikes, then he caught a curveball and sent it into the bleachers. Boston was ahead, 2-0.

In the Yankee half of the fifth inning, two pinstripes got on base. Derek Jeter stepped up with two outs and a chance to score some runs. But Pedro threw a strike. Then he got Jeter to swing and miss on a high fastball—strike two! Pedro next threw a ball off the plate. Then he threw his fastball. Strike three!

Pedro was out of the inning, and went on to win in a 2-0 shutout. After the game, Pedro acknowledged that he could no longer produce the 97-mile-an-hour fastball all the time, and everyone knew the now 32-year-old player couldn't throw much more than a hundred pitches a game. "I'm a more mature pitcher," he said. "I pitch to my strengths. If I pitch to my strengths velocity isn't important. I think I can be consistently 93, 92, 91. If you do that then velocity is just a number."[84]

Boston had won six of the first seven games against the Yankees, and the Red Sox, who had come in second place behind the Yankees the past six years in a row, were now in first place—4½ games ahead of the hapless and hated Yankees.

Except . . . not so fast.

In June, the Red Sox began a West Coast trip by losing to

the Anaheim Angels, while the Yankees beat the Baltimore Orioles. The next day, Pedro started against the Angels and gave up seven runs in a losing effort. There was just one bright spot in the game for Pedro. In the third inning, he logged the 2,500th strikeout of his career. Only 25 pitchers had reached that milestone in the history of major league baseball, just a handful of them current players: teammate Curt Schilling, along with Cy Young Award winners Greg Maddux, Randy Johnson, and Roger Clemens.

It is a very exclusive club.

When the month ended, the Red Sox were $5^1/_2$ games *behind* the Yankees in the standings. The Red Sox landed in New York for a three-game series and promptly lost the first two. Boston's Johnny Damon said, "I don't know if it's The Curse or The Ghost, but things aren't going our way. Right now, the Yankees are in the driver's seat."[85]

Added Pedro Martinez, who was scheduled to pitch the third game: "The Yankees might run away with it. But we could still beat them as the wild card. I still think we have the better team, no matter what their record is."[86]

It was up to Pedro to try to stop the Yankees. Unfortunately, he couldn't quite do it. The game was tied at 3-3 when Pedro left in the seventh. It was still tied after nine. In the thirteenth inning, Manny Ramirez slammed a home run for Boston, putting the Red Sox ahead, 4-3. But the Yankees had that last at-bat. A single, and then a double, and then *another* double brought in two runs and won the game for the pinstripes.

Now the Yankees were pulling further ahead, and the Red Sox were battling with several other contenders for the American League wild-card spot. It looked like Boston would have its usual season—starting out strong, faltering at the end, losing to the Yankees.

At the end of July, the Yankees came to Fenway Park for a three-game series against the backdrop of the Democratic National Convention. Curt Schilling pitched the first game for

Boston and gave up five runs in the sixth inning. The Red Sox went down, 8-7. The Red Sox literally battled back to take the second game, as a fight broke out, and then they scored three runs in the ninth to outlast the Yankees, 11-10. The final game, when presidential candidate and Boston native son John Kerry threw out the ceremonial first pitch, went to the Red Sox, 9-6, and put some hope back in Red Sox Nation.

Could the Red Sox turn it around? The very next night, Pedro led the effort, posting a win against the Baltimore Orioles.

Then on August 7, Pedro struck out 11 batters in seven innings as Boston beat the Detroit Tigers, 7-4.

On August 12, Pedro pitched a full nine innings and shut out the Tampa Bay Devil Rays, 6-0.

On August 17, Pedro went seven innings against the Toronto Blue Jays. This time he was not perfect and gave up four runs, but the Red Sox still won the day, 5-4.

Pedro pitched against the Tigers again on August 28, allowing four hits and one run in seven innings. The Red Sox took the game, 5-1.

The Red Sox were back. They were not going to catch the Yankees, who were still $5^1/_2$ games ahead, but for the second year in a row, and the fourth time since Pedro had joined the team, the Red Sox would win the wild-card slot—and have a chance at the grand prize.

The Red Sox winning streak continued into September. On September 3, the Texas Rangers came to town. Pedro struck out nine in seven innings—and Manny Ramirez hit his thirty-seventh home run—helping the Sox win their tenth game in a row.

"I had good command of every pitch," said Martinez after the game. "I'm pretty happy with the way everything went. Right now, I'm in good shape. I'm at a tip-top point in my game." Speaking of the team, he went on to say, "The way we are rolling right now, we are coming, and we are coming hard . . . Everybody kept saying, 'When is this team going to go on a

In the months of August and September 2004, the Red Sox went 39-17
to earn the franchise's most wins (98) since they won 99 games in 1978.
During this stretch, Boston put together a 10-game winning streak, which
included a 2-0 win by Pedro Martinez over the Texas Rangers on
September 3.

streak?' A lot of these guys saw something in this team that
really made you believe that we had the potential to actually
break out. At this time, I feel great, and I thank God for it. I
hope I can keep feeling this same way."[87]

Nothing lasts forever, though, and the Boston streak ended
in a loss to Texas on September 4. The Red Sox went on to lose
a few more in September, including a game in New York, when
the Yankees pummeled Pedro for eight earned runs on their
way to an 11-1 rout.

Then, at the end of the season, the Yankees went to Boston

for a three-game series. Pedro gave up two early runs in the first game. But after seven innings, he had a one-run lead.

Normally, Pedro would come out after seven innings, having done his part. Manager Francona, however, in a move eerily reminiscent of the prior year's Game 7, sent a tired Pedro trudging back to the mound in the eighth. Sure enough, the leadoff Yankee batter stroked a home run to tie the game. Then Pedro threw to Bernie Williams, who smacked a double. A single brought in Williams and put the Yankees ahead, 5-4.

Francona finally went to the mound, amidst a chorus of boos from Red Sox fans. He relieved Pedro, but it was too late. The game ended with the Yankees on top, 6-4.

"I made some pretty good pitches . . . what can I say?" said a somber Martinez after the game, his third straight loss. "Just tip my hat and call the Yankees my daddy. I can't find a way to beat them at this point. They're that good right now, that hot—against me at least."[88]

Some people blamed Francona for leaving Pedro in too long, just like Grady Little had done in 2003. But Pedro only blamed himself, saying there was no reason to be upset with Francona.

Added a defensive Francona: "If I thought he was losing it, I would have taken him out. In my opinion he still had good stuff. I wouldn't have left him in if I thought he was out of gas. I thought he was going to go out and get them out. I thought he was in command of what he was doing. I thought he deserved to stay out there."[89]

Battle-hardened veterans that they were, the Red Sox took the last two regular season games against the Yankees, which gave them the edge in their 2004 matchups, 11-8. Still, none of that mattered anymore. What seemed obvious at the beginning of September is what actually happened by the end of September. The Yankees had won the division. For the seventh year in a row, the Red Sox came in second. This year, like the previous year, they earned the wild-card position—and would be headed for the playoffs.

THE POSSIBLE DREAM

It was Curt Schilling who started the ALDS for the Red Sox, against the Anaheim Angels. Boston hitters made things easy in the fourth inning, when they rallied for seven runs, and the Red Sox took the opener, 9-3.

Game 2 of this short, best-of-five series pitted Pedro against fellow Dominican Bartolo Colon of the Angels. The Red Sox loaded the bases in the first inning but failed to score. They loaded the bases again in the second, and this time took a 1-0 lead when Manny Ramirez drew a two-out walk from Colon.

The Angels scored one right back with a walk and two singles. Then in the fifth, Martinez loaded the bases and gave up a two-run single. But after seven innings, Pedro left the game with a 4-3 lead and was credited with the win. "I'm really happy to go back to where I wanted to be and do the things I wanted to do," said Martinez after the game. "Thank God I turned it around."[90]

Two days later, a towering David Ortiz home run gave Boston the third game, 8-6, and the Red Sox swept the series 3-0. The fans went wild, the Boston locker room celebrated, and Pedro donned a T-shirt that read: WHY NOT US?

With that the Boston Red Sox earned the chance at redemption against the Yankees, who beat the Minnesota Twins in the other division series.

The battle would begin on October 12, 2004, in Yankee Stadium.

Curt Schilling started the game for Boston with a sore ankle, and the Yankees beat him up for eight runs. The Red Sox did nothing until the seventh. Then they exploded for seven runs. But it wasn't enough, as the Yankees went on to win, 10-7.

Game 2. New York City. Pedro Martinez scheduled to pitch. The headline on the back page of the New York *Daily News*, referring to Pedro's end-of-September remark, challenged: "Come to Daddy!" Hawkers sold T-shirts that sneered: "Hey Red Sox . . . Who's Your Daddy?"

Pedro's teammate David Ortiz laughed off the taunts. "I don't think Pedro has a daddy anymore. Whatever he's been doing, he's at the top of his game. That's the Pedro everyone knows, the one who pitched the last couple of starts."[91]

When Pedro took the mound in Yankee Stadium—amid chants of "Who's Your Da-dee? Who's Your Da-dee?"—he opened the game by throwing six straight balls. But he soon settled down and pitched into the sixth inning, striking out seven and giving up only four hits. Unfortunately, his performance just wasn't good enough, as those four hits resulted in three runs for the Yankees. The Red Sox produced only two hits all day. The Yankees won Game 2, by a score of 3-1.

Asked about the fans who chanted "Who's Your Daddy?" Pedro responded: "It actually made me feel really, really good. I . . . felt like somebody important, because I caught the attention of 60,000 fans, plus the whole world, watching a guy that is . . . you reverse the time back 15 years ago, I was sitting under a mango tree without 50 cents to pay for a bus. And today, I was the center of attention of the whole city of New York. I thank God for that, and you know what? I don't regret one bit what they do out there."[92]

Still, the Red Sox were going to Fenway Park, down 2-0 in the best-of-seven series. The first day back, another nail was hammered into the Red Sox coffin. The Yankees teed off on Boston pitchers and quickly got into double digits. The final score: 19-8. As famous author and Red Sox fan Stephen King pointed out sourly: "Replace the hyphen with a 1 and you have the last year the Red Sox won the World Series."[93]

Now there's a horror of a thought!

But, as an old-time Yankees catcher was reported to have said: It ain't over till it's over.

With their backs to the wall, the Red Sox came out and did battle. In Game 4, the Yankees went ahead early, 2-0. Then Boston scored three runs in the fifth inning to take the lead, 3-2. A triple and a couple of singles brought in two Yankee runs in the sixth to put the pinstripes back on top, 4-3. The Red Sox squeezed a run in the ninth inning to stay alive, and the contest went to extra frames.

In the eleventh, the Yankees filled the bases, but they couldn't score. In the twelfth, Boston put a man on base. Then David Ortiz stepped to the plate and drilled a line drive over the right field fence for a home run. The Red Sox were saved. At 5 hours and 2 minutes, it was the longest game ever played in postseason history.

Now down 3-1, instead of 3-0, it was again Pedro's turn to take the mound—and now *this* game was destined to become the longest game ever played in the annals of postseason baseball, at 14 innings, and 5 hours and 49 minutes.

The Red Sox scored two in the very first inning to take the lead. But Pedro gave up a home run to Bernie Williams in the second. Red Sox 2, Yankees 1.

Pedro allowed two base runners in both the third and fourth innings, but no one scored. In the sixth, Pedro gave up two singles. Then he hit a batter. With two outs and the bases loaded, Pedro pitched to Derek Jeter, who flicked a hit down the right-field line, which cleared the bases. Suddenly it was 4-2 Yankees.

Pedro kept going. He hit another batter and walked another to load the bases again. Finally, he got Hideki Matsui to line out to Trot Nixon to end the inning. After six innings, Pedro was done for the day.

Before the game was over, six more Boston pitchers would take the mound to stem the Yankee tide. All together they succeeded, while Pedro's countryman David Ortiz knocked a homer in the eighth to close the gap to 4-3. Later in the inning, another Boston run crossed the plate to tie the game at 4-4.

Again, it would be an extra-inning marathon, with runners getting on base but no one scoring—until finally, in the fourteenth, Johnny Damon drew a walk. Then Manny Ramirez walked. Next up, David Ortiz—Big Papi—and, you guessed it, he lined a ball to center field for a hit. Damon rushed home. And the Red Sox—they won again!

No team in baseball had ever come back from a 3-0 deficit to win a postseason series. But when the momentum changes, sometimes it changes dramatically. Now, down 3-2, the Red Sox were on a roll. Curt Schilling went out to pitch Game 6 in Yankee Stadium and shut down the Yankees. A late-inning Yankee rally was squelched when Alex Rodriguez batted the ball out of the first baseman's glove and was called safe, then ruled out. With that, Yankee hopes faltered and Boston took the game, 4-2.

The final chapter was played out in Yankee Stadium, with Kevin Brown starting for the pinstripes. But Boston hitters made quick work of Brown, batting out a truckload of hits, including three home runs, and won the game, 10-3. The Boston comeback was complete—the biggest in major league history.

Yet, to reverse the Curse completely, the Red Sox would also have to win the World Series, and a couple of days later, the National League champions, the St. Louis Cardinals, came to Fenway Park. Game 1 was a slugfest that went 11-9 in the Red Sox favor. The Red Sox took Game 2 easily, by a score of 6-2.

Boston was ahead in the series, 2-0. But in 1986, the Red Sox took the first two games of the World Series against the New York Mets—and Boston went on to lose in seven games. It ain't over till it's over.

The series went to St. Louis for Game 3, with Pedro Martinez pitching his first-ever World Series start—the day after his 33rd birthday. Without a new contract, it might also be the last game Pedro would ever pitch for the Red Sox.

Manny Ramirez hit a home run in the Boston half of the first inning to give the Red Sox a quick lead. Then Pedro came out and gave up a walk. Then an infield hit. Then another walk to load the bases, with one out. Pedro got the next Cardinal hitter to pop to shallow center, and Manny Ramirez threw a perfect strike to home plate to get the runner trying to score from third base. Inning over.

Pedro Martinez holds the World Series Championship trophy above his head after Boston's 3-0 win over the St. Louis Cardinals in Game 4 of the 2004 World Series. The Red Sox swept the Cardinals, 4-0, to win their first World Series since 1918.

After his shaky start, Pedro went on to throw like his old self. He retired the last 14 batters he faced, striking out the last two. He pitched seven scoreless innings, while Boston put three runs across, and so he left the mound with the game well in hand. As he came into the dugout, his teammates circled round and engulfed him in hugs.

"There's a lot of career left in him. I'm not surprised by anything I saw tonight," said an impressed Curt Schilling after the game. "It was a phenomenal performance, phenomenal. He was unbelievable. They had one shot and they missed, and he ran with it after that."[94]

Boston won Game 3 by a score of 4-1, and the next day closed out the series with a 3-0 victory, to win the World Series for the first time in 86 years. Champagne flowed in the Boston clubhouse, and cheers went up all across Red Sox Nation. As for Pedro Martinez, he described the moment—after seven years with the Red Sox—as the pinnacle of his career. "This is just a great moment of satisfaction," he said after the game, with a Dominican Republic flag draped over his shoulders. "Just being able to bring it to Boston is the maximum. I couldn't express it. We are the champions."[95]

8

New Face of the Mets

Seven years after landing in Boston on that cold December evening in 1997 to sign a deal with the Red Sox, Pedro Martinez took another flight from his home in the Dominican Republic. This time his destination was New York City.

Pedro had rejected an offer worth $40.5 million to stay in Boston. Why? The Red Sox management had at first only wanted to sign him for an additional two years. Then they reluctantly agreed to three. But Pedro felt that Boston was not really committed to him, while other teams were dangling better offers. The St. Louis Cardinals wanted him. The Yankees had expressed some interest.

But it was a fellow countryman from the Dominican Republic, a man named Omar Minaya, who finally landed a deal with Pedro.

Minaya had become general manager of the New York Mets in September 2004, after spending 20 years working his way up the baseball-management ladder. The Mets had been near the bottom of the National League standings for three years running, and he was

After seven seasons in Boston, Pedro Martinez signed a four-year, $54 million contract with the New York Mets during the 2004 off-season. Martinez is flanked here by New York Mets General Manager Omar Minaya (left) and Manager Willie Randolph.

hired to reinvigorate the team, put the Mets in a position to challenge the Yankees as New York's favorite team, and maybe even eventually win the World Series. The Mets had made it to the World Series in 2000 but lost to the Yankees. The last time they won the championship was in 1986, against the Boston Red Sox.

Minaya had flown down to Santo Domingo over Thanksgiving to have lunch with Pedro, who now lives in a walled compound located a few miles from the New York Mets baseball camp in the Dominican Republic. Minaya told Pedro he wanted him on his team. Minaya later explained, "We got to looking at each other, got to focusing on the bigger picture. I said, 'Pedro, you know what? We're the Mets. We're not supposed to win. So why don't you just think we're David and we're going to have to fight Goliath?' I said, 'Hey, look, me and you have been David all our lives.' That's how we connected."[96]

Minaya figured if Pedro came to the Mets, the star pitcher might attract other top talent to New York's National League team—just as he had done in Boston by easing the way for Manny Ramirez and David Ortiz to sign with the Red Sox. There was something else, too. Minaya was Hispanic. He wanted to offer opportunities to Latin players in New York and give the city's large Hispanic population a team to root for. Pedro would be the new face of the Mets.

OMAR MINAYA'S NOT-SO-SECRET PLAN

The New York Mets went to the World Series in 2000 (and lost to the Yankees), but over the next four years, the team went downhill fast. Finally, the Mets' owners decided to do something drastic—they hired Omar Minaya as general manager of the team at the end of the 2004 season.

Minaya is a local boy. He grew up in Queens, New York, within shouting distance of Shea Stadium. But he was born in a town called Valverde on the northern side of the Dominican Republic, opposite Santo Domingo. His family moved to Queens in 1967, when Omar was eight years old.

A star baseball player as a kid, Omar earned a minor league contract. But he wasn't good enough for the major leagues—he only lasted two years before calling it quits. He landed a job with the Texas Rangers as a scout, looking for prospects in his native Dominican Republic. Omar made his name when he discovered Sammy Sosa, who went on to become a top slugger for the Chicago Cubs.

In 1997, Minaya accepted an assistant's job with the New York Mets. Then, in 2002, he took a gamble: He signed on as the general manager of the Montreal Expos and thus became the first Latino to run a major league ball club. He only got the job because nobody else wanted it—the Expos were destined for

For his part, Pedro saw right away that he would be getting more respect—and a better deal—in New York than he would in Boston, or anyplace else for that matter. So the pitcher, now 33 years old, agreed to sign with the "other" team from New York. The contract would keep him in the Big Apple for four years—through the 2008 season—and award him $54 million. Believe it or not, Pedro was actually taking a pay cut to join the Mets, from $17 million in 2004 to an average of $13.5 million in New York.

On December 15, 2004, Pedro arrived in New York and went to the hospital for a complete physical, along with a

extinction (they were transformed into the Washington Nationals in 2005).

When Omar Minaya took over as Mets general manager, he had several objectives. One was to ensure the team had a strong leader by hiring a new manager. For that he went across town to sign up Willie Randolph, longtime coach with the New York Yankees. Then Minaya needed to make a bold stroke to bring some talent, and some excitement, to the team. Hence, Minaya's Thanksgiving trip to Santo Domingo.

Just as Pedro had attracted other Latin stars like Manny Ramirez and David Ortiz to Boston, Pedro now gave the New York Mets credibility with Latin players. Soon Minaya was flying to Puerto Rico to talk to All-Star center fielder Carlos Beltran—and suddenly, Beltran was also in the fold.

The Mets are still not World Series contenders. Omar Minaya has more work to do. For now, though, the Dominican flags are waving in Shea Stadium, especially on the nights when Pedro pitches. The team boasts up-and-coming Latin players like fellow Dominican, shortstop Jose Reyes. Before Omar and Pedro are finished, there might just be another World Series victory to celebrate.

thorough exam of his sometimes-aching right shoulder. Omar Minaya was no fool—he wanted to make sure he was investing in a sound arm. Pedro passed the physical, and the next day went out to Shea Stadium, in the Flushing, Queens, section of New York City for a press conference announcing his agreement to join the team.

The three-time Cy Young Award winner donned Mets jersey No. 45. Omar Minaya told the crowd: "We got a guy who transcends wins and losses. We are trying to build a championship team here and for me it's about bringing players from within the system. We today made a statement . . . [There are] major league players that have called me since the signing and said, 'Hey, I want to be a Met. I want to be a Met.' . . . But what's also important to me, that kid we don't know about, that [future] Pedro Martinez that you don't know about, that I don't know about, that might be in the Dominican Republic or Venezuela, that kid's father and that kid, you know what he wants to be today? He wants to be a Met. That's the value of Pedro Martinez."[97]

As for Pedro, he simply explained to the people at Shea Stadium, "Omar showed me respect and commitment."[98]

As he stood there, the press and sports fans around New York couldn't help but recall how Pedro, who had won 117 games during his time in Boston, while losing only 37, had for seven years kept the Red Sox in playoff contention and finally helped the team win the World Series. "Remember, Boston was there for 86 years and it seemed like it was going to be there forever," Pedro told his audience. "And I can proudly say that I was part of the team that won it for Boston. And I want to do the same thing here."[99]

As everyone knew, that was just the tip of the Martinez iceberg. In his 12-year major league career up to that point, with the Dodgers, the Expos, and the Red Sox, his total won-loss record was 182-76. He had posted a career ERA of 2.71—the lowest among active pitchers in the major leagues.

Everyone also knew that the numbers didn't tell the whole story of Pedro as a baseball player. "There is a feeling that comes with coming to the park when Pedro is going to pitch," said former teammate Johnny Damon. "You never know what is going to happen, but you don't want to miss it. Pedro is one of the greatest pitchers in the game. When he's on the mound, you might see something you'll never forget."[100]

No one would doubt that Pedro was destined for the Hall of Fame, and no one could forget Pedro's impact on baseball, even beyond the numbers. There was the perfect game that he brought into extra innings against the San Diego Padres in 1995, retiring 27 batters in a row, before giving up a hit in the tenth and settling for a shutout. There was the 1996 pitching duel against his brother Ramon of the Los Angeles Dodgers, the game that the older brother won in the end.

There was the first Cy Young Award in 1997. The record-breaking contract with the Boston Red Sox. Then the second and third Cy Young Awards in 1999 and 2000.

Who could forget the rivalry with the Yankees and long road to the World Series that involved the September 1999 outing against New York, when Pedro struck out a record 17 Yankees in one game? Or later that season, Pedro's heroic appearance after he'd been injured, when he pitched six innings of no-hit ball to earn the win in the final game for Boston in the playoffs against the Cleveland Indians?

Then there was the face-off against Yankee coach Don Zimmer, and the unfortunate Game 7 in 2003, when Boston manager Grady Little left a tiring Pedro on the mound. Ultimately, there was victory over the Yankees, and then the St. Louis Cardinals, and the crowning achievement of the World Series after 86 years of struggle and frustration.

Said Pedro's friend—and now former teammate—Manny Ramirez: "Pedro's going to be the best thing they ever seen, man. We're talking about one of the greatest pitchers of all time. They're going to be very happy they got him."[101]

ON THE MOUND IN NEW YORK

Cut to the middle of the 2005 season. Pedro has once again been elected to the All-Star team—his third time in the National League (including twice with the Montreal Expos, in 1996 and 1997) and his seventh time overall. Just as he had done eight years earlier in Boston, Pedro was burning up the league. The headlines read:

Pedro Brings Backs Glory Days at Shea
Martinez Mania Sweeps Flushing
Pedro Powers Mets to Victory
Pedro Dazzles Home Fans

Of course, "Pobody's Nerfect," as they say. In June, the Seattle Mariners managed to do something they hadn't been able to accomplish in seven years: They beat Pedro Martinez, who until June 18, 2005, had a 13-0 record against the team. "He's a great pitcher, and obviously he's dominated us over the years," commented Mariners starter Ryan Franklin. "We didn't really hit the ball that hard off him, but we had some seeing-eye ground balls that got through some holes, and that was pretty much the game."[102]

Meanwhile, Pedro has supplied some fireworks at Shea Stadium. Fans ask: When is Pedro pitching? Then they rush out and buy their tickets. When he's on the mound, the stands are more crowded, the fans more enthusiastic. Some have even suggested that the team plays better when Pedro is pitching.

Starting out at Shea Stadium, the 33-year-old pitcher no longer had quite the velocity he had when he first arrived in the majors. He could no longer throw 98-mile-an-hour fastballs. But he could still routinely throw them at 90 miles an hour and get to 94 in a pinch. More importantly, Pedro has retained and even improved his command over the location of his pitches—he can hit the inside corner for a strike, or throw low and out-side, close enough so the batter *thinks* it is a strike. Also, and as always, his pitches move around, they dance on their way to the

plate, they break at the last moment and end up where the batter least expects them.

Furthermore, Pedro is a master of the setup. He lulls a batter into thinking the next pitch is going to be a fastball. Then
he throws a change-up—or the other way around.

He still has his three consistent strikeout pitches: the fastball, the curveball, and the change-up. These days, though, his
arm does tire. As he has learned from bitter experience, he is at
his best if he calls it a day at around a hundred pitches. After
that, his delivery suffers. But his performance takes the Mets
into the seventh or eighth inning, and if the team gets any hits
at all, then there's usually a win.

Pedro is not above a little gamesmanship. He still will
throw inside at a batter to challenge him—to make sure the
opponent doesn't lean into the plate and get too comfortable.
He'll pull other little tricks as well. For example, in a May 2005
game against the Florida Marlins, Pedro wore the short sleeves
on his shirt a little longer than usual. Longer sleeves mask the
movement of his arm, just slightly. He also wore a dark-colored
long-sleeved undershirt—with the left sleeve cut off. Again, the
dark color made his arm less visible during the night game—
as it came over his head to make the pitch—while leaving the
hitters to wonder: What's Pedro doing with one long sleeve and
one short one?

The Marlins, who boasted the best batting average in the
National League, protested his unusual undershirt. Eventually,
he was forced to slide a sleeve onto his left arm as well. But it
didn't matter. Pedro pitched eight innings of shutout ball and
won the game anyway.

When the Marlins finally did threaten, in the seventh
inning, with a man on third and one out, Pedro struck out
Marlins batter Juan Encarnacion on a big breaking curveball.
Then he faced Mike Lowell. He threw him five curveballs in a
row, which brought the count to 3-2. Later on, Pedro explained
what happened next. "He had to be thinking, 'There's no way
he'll throw another breaking ball.' So I decided I had to throw

(continued on page 115)

THE LIGHTER SIDE OF PEDRO

When he ascends the mound, Pedro levels his dark brown eyes down toward the plate and stares menacingly at opposing hitters. Then he begins throwing his repertoire of pitches that intimidate, brush back, puzzle, and sometimes completely baffle hitters.

On days when he's not pitching, though, Pedro presents a different face to the world—sometimes literally. During one game in Boston, Pedro donned a Yoda (the Jedi Master from *Star Wars*) mask and roamed around the Red Sox dugout. At another outing, during batting practice at a game against the Seattle Mariners, he fixed two seagull feathers to the back of his hat and started shagging fly balls in the outfield.

The fact is, when he's not on the mound, Pedro likes to clown around. He blows big bubbles with chewing gum and puts them up on the top of the dugout steps. For Pedro, they represent a big zero—for the number of runs he thinks the opposing team is going to score. Pedro also has fun imitating other pitchers and batters, and generally keeps up a patter to calm everyone's nerves and help his teammates stay loose. Once, in 1999, his teammates jokingly tied him to a pole at the stadium—and threatened to leave him there until he shut up!

Sometimes Pedro will stand on the top step of the dugout and watch the opposing pitcher; he might pick up a habit or peculiarity about the pitcher that he can pass on to the hitters and perhaps help them out. Or, just by his very presence there, he might distract or otherwise intimidate the opposing team's pitcher, once again giving an edge to his own teammates.

"I think it's great," Dan Duquette, the former general manager of the Red Sox once said of Pedro's antics. "It keeps the players loose. Pedro is all business on the days he pitches, and he's all for the team on the days he doesn't."*

Pedro's personality sometimes shows through on the field as well. During one game in June 2005, against the Arizona

When not pitching, Pedro Martinez often likes to clown around and have a good time. Martinez is pictured here wearing a Yoda (the Jedi Master from *Star Wars*) mask during the 1998 season.

Diamondbacks, the sprinkler system at Shea Stadium accidentally went off during the first inning. While the umpires and the other players fled to dry ground, Pedro calmly walked over and put his face in the spray. "Water is a blessing," he said later, "and I got wet."**

Mets manager Willie Randolph was amused by his pitcher's antics. He called him "a showman," and smiled and commented, "It's Pedro being Pedro."***

Pedro has said that he's never experienced any racism. "We don't have a color in our country. In our country, what we have in mind is how you are as a person and that's what we care about."†

Meanwhile, his favorite movies? They've been reported as: *Titanic*, *The Passion of the Christ*, and *Shrek*. He has said his favorite actor is Harrison Ford. But if anyone ever makes a movie of his life, Pedro said he wants actor Denzel Washington to play him.

Back on the field, when a fielder makes a great catch or an inning-ending play, Pedro will typically raise his head and give a kiss to the sky—as if to thank God for blessing him with the opportunity to be on the mound. Later in that June 2005 Diamondbacks game when the sprinkler went off, Mets right fielder Mike Cameron made a great running catch in the sixth inning, tripping and falling to the ground as he stuck out his glove and—surprising everyone, including himself—snagged the fly ball. After the crowd roared in appreciation of the fielder's gymnastics, Pedro faced toward Cameron and bowed, as if to thank his teammate for saving the day. With that motion, Pedro caused the crowd to roar again—once more proving that every time Pedro pitches, it's an event.

Mets general manager Omar Minaya sums up: "There's just an energy to him—and to us and everyone who comes—on days he pitches. He makes excitement. Not many pitchers do that. He's so focused. And he throws pitches that wow everyone . . . No one has it like Pedro has it."††

* "Baseball; Martinez Fast with a Laugh," *Boston Herald*, September 2, 1998.

** Marty Noble, "Pedro at Top of His Game in Mets' Win," *www.mlb.com*, June 3, 2005.

*** Ibid.

† Dan Shaughnessy, "A Conversation with Pedro Martinez," *Boston Globe*, October 3, 1999.

†† Marty Noble, "Pedro at Top of His Game," *www.mlb.com*, June 3, 2005.

(*continued from page 111*)

one that looked like a fastball."[103] Pedro then dealt his breaking ball once again. Lowell swung and missed the ball that curved off the plate outside.

"How could he be ready for that pitch?" asked Mets outfielder Mike Cameron, with sympathy for the baffled Lowell. "No one throws pitches like Pedro."[104] The Mets took the game, 1-0. Pedro's 2005 record at that point went to 5-1.

Less than two weeks later, Pedro set the Shea Stadium crowd abuzz when he pitched through five innings, then six innings of no-hit baseball. No one in Mets history has pitched a no-hitter. The fans were on their feet, chanting "Pe-dro! Pe-dro!" as they began to think he might be the first to do it in this game against the Houston Astros. "I didn't really realize it until I heard the fans clapping," Martinez said in a postgame interview. "I never look at the scoreboard. I look everywhere else. It's not the first time that's happened to me."[105]

In the seventh inning, Houston rookie Chris Burke took a swing at a Martinez curveball and sent it over the left-field fence. It was Burke's first major league home run. With that homer, he squelched Pedro's no-hitter—much to the disappointment of Mets fans cheering him on. Pedro completed the game, winning 3-1. He struck out 12 batters, including a K for all three Astro hitters in the ninth inning. Fittingly, it was spoiler Chris Burke who went down as Pedro's last victim.

Pedro continues his career, carding a 15-8 record for the 2005 season and working his way toward 3,000 career strikeouts, a number only a handful of major league pitchers have achieved. The Mets were much improved in 2005—finishing with a record of 83 and 79. That was not good enough for even the wild-card position, and so the "other" team from New York was not destined to play its way into the postseason quite yet.

But who knows? It took Pedro seven years to get the Red Sox to the World Series. Maybe he can do it for the Mets in four.

Chronology and Timeline

1492   Christopher Columbus discovers the island of Hispaniola.

1918   The Boston Red Sox, led by Babe Ruth, win the World Series.

1971   On October 25, Pedro Jaime Martinez is born in the Dominican Republic.

1988   Older brother Ramon Martinez joins the Los Angeles Dodgers pitching staff; Pedro signs minor league contract with the team.

1990   Pedro moves to the United States to join rookie team in Great Falls, Montana.

1992   Pedro called up to the major leagues in September, joining brother Ramon on the Los Angeles Dodgers' pitching staff.

1993   Pedro traded to Montreal Expos in November.

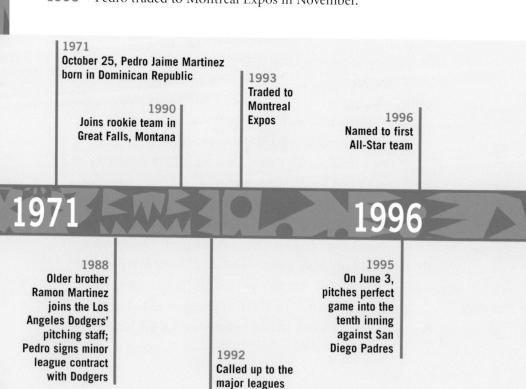

1971
October 25, Pedro Jaime Martinez born in Dominican Republic

1990
Joins rookie team in Great Falls, Montana

1993
Traded to Montreal Expos

1996
Named to first All-Star team

1971   1996

1988
Older brother Ramon Martinez joins the Los Angeles Dodgers' pitching staff; Pedro signs minor league contract with Dodgers

1992
Called up to the major leagues

1995
On June 3, pitches perfect game into the tenth inning against San Diego Padres

1995   On June 3, Pedro pitches perfect game into the tenth inning against San Diego Padres.

1996   Pedro voted to his first All-Star Game; on August 29, Pedro, pitching for the Expos, starts against Ramon, pitching for the Dodgers—Pedro strikes out 12 batters but loses to his brother, 2-1.

1997   Wins National League Cy Young Award in November; signs record contract with Boston Red Sox in December.

1998   On April 11, Pedro pitches first game for Red Sox at Fenway Park to multiple standing ovations; Boston loses in ALDS to Cleveland, 3-2, when manager leaves Pedro on the bench.

1999   Older brother Ramon joins Pedro on the Red Sox pitching staff; Pedro named All-Star Most Valuable Player; on September 10, Pedro strikes out a record 17 Yankees; in October, Pedro hurts right shoulder, comes back to win

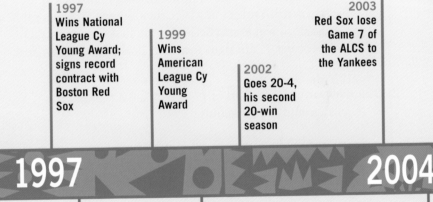

1997
Wins National League Cy Young Award; signs record contract with Boston Red Sox

1999
Wins American League Cy Young Award

2002
Goes 20-4, his second 20-win season

2003
Red Sox lose Game 7 of the ALCS to the Yankees

1997   2004

2000
Wins third Cy Young Award

2004
Boston wins World Series for the first time in 86 years; Signs four-year deal with New York Mets

1998
Pitches first game for Red Sox at Fenway Park

ALDS Game 5 against Cleveland Indians; goes 23-4 and wins American League Cy Young Award.

2000   Wins third Cy Young Award.

2001   Pedro on disabled list with sore shoulder.

2002   Pedro chalks up a 20-4 record, his second 20-win season.

2003   Red Sox exercise option for Pedro to pitch one more year; on October 6, Pedro wins fifth and deciding ALDS game against Oakland; on October 11, Pedro has famous scuffle with Yankee coach Don Zimmer; on October 16, Manager Grady Little leaves in a tiring Martinez and Yankees come back to win Game 7 of ALCS by a score of 6-5.

2004   In August, Pedro and Boston go on a tear and bolster their confidence while threatening the Yankees; in September, Pedro makes "Yankees my daddy" comment after losing to New York; Pedro wins Game 2 and Red Sox sweep Anaheim Angels in ALDS; Boston makes dramatic come-back to defeat Yankees in ALCS, then sweeps St. Louis Cardinals to win World Series for the first time in 86 years; in December, Pedro signs four-year deal with the New York Mets.

2005   Posts won-loss record of 15-8, with a 2.82 earned run average and 208 strikeouts.

Notes

Chapter 1

1 "Baseball—Martinez Lands in Boston, Happy and Enthusiastic," *Seattle Times*, December 12, 1997.

2 Ibid.; also: "Red Sox Sign Martinez," *Chicago Sun Times*, December 12, 1997.

3 "Martinez Heads to Boston," *Vancouver Sun*, December 13, 1997; also: "Baseball; Martinez: I Didn't Do It for the Money," *Boston Herald*, December 13, 1997.

4 "Baseball—Martinez, Boston's Latest Catch, Speaks Glowingly of New Team, Fans, Fenway," *Seattle Times*, December 2, 1997.

5 "Martinez Again Baffles Mets," *Bergen Evening Record*, April 27, 1997.

6 "Martinez Needs Streak to Boost Cy Young Bid: Sure Other Stats Are Great, But Won-Lost Is Key," *Montreal Gazette*, August 24, 1997.

7 "Only the Yanks Stand between Mets and Martinez," *New York Times*, November 5, 1997.

8 "Baseball; Pedro Keeps It Personal; Red Sox Star Says Riches Won't Spoil Him," *Boston Herald*, December 3, 1997.

9 Jim Gallagher, *Latinos in Baseball: Ramon Martinez* (Childs, Md.: Mitchell Lane Publishers, 2000), 41.

10 "Martinez Has A's Looking Like April Fools," *Sacramento Bee*, April 2, 1998.

11 "Martinez Regains Dominating Form," *Buffalo News*, September 30, 1998.

Chapter 2

12 Jim Gallagher, *Latinos in Baseball: Pedro Martinez* (Childs, Md.: Mitchell Lane Publishers, 1999), 15; also: Gallagher, *Latinos in Baseball: Ramon Martinez*, 12.

13 Gallagher, *Latinos in Baseball: Ramon Martinez*, 12.

14 Ibid., 12.

15 Gallagher, *Latinos in Baseball: Pedro Martinez*, 15; also: A.R. Schaefer, *Sports Heroes: Pedro Martinez* (Mankato, Minn.: Capstone High-Interest Books, 2003), 13; also, Associated Press, May 8, 1998.

16 Gallagher, *Latinos in Baseball: Ramon Martinez*, 13.

17 Gallagher, *Latinos in Baseball: Pedro Martinez*, 17; also: Biography Resource Center—*www.galegroup.com*—Pedro Martinez in Sports Stars, Series 5. U*X*L, 1999.

18 Ibid.

19 Matt McHale, "Pedro Martinez Lightens Dodgers' Mood Despite Loss, Rookie Sparkles Against Reds," *Orange County Register*, October 1, 1992.

20 Ibid.

Chapter 3

21 Randy Franz, "Dodgers Update," *Orange County Register*, April 10, 1993.

22 Franz, "Braves' Pitching Silences Dodgers," *Orange County Register*, April 12, 1993.

23 Gallagher, *Latinos in Baseball: Ramon Martinez*, 25.

24 Ian MacDonald, "Same Old Hurler Martinez; but Added Curve Can Make Him Overpowering," *Montreal Gazette*, April 8, 1994.

25 Gallagher, *Latinos in Baseball: Pedro Martinez*, 30.

26 Lawrence Rocca, "Brothers Dreading Matchup," *Orange County Register*, August 29, 1996.

27 Rocca, "Dodgers Prevail on Brothers' Day," *Orange County Register*, August 30, 1996.

28 "Dodgers Win Battle of Brothers in Arms; Ramon Martinez Outpitches Pedro in Wild-Card Race," *Ottawa Citizen*, August 30, 1996.

29 Gallagher, *Latinos in Baseball: Pedro Martinez*, 34; also: Gallagher, *Latinos in Baseball: Ramon Martinez*, 35.

30 Gallagher, *Latinos in Baseball: Ramon Martinez*, 35.

Chapter 4

31 Stephen Krasner, *Pedro Martinez* (Philadelphia, Pa.: Chelsea House Publishers, 2002), 41.

32 Richard Justice, "Martinez Is Hometown Hero; Red Sox Starter Fans 5 of 6, Named MVP," *Washington Post*, July 14, 1999.

33 Buster Olney, "1 Hit, 17 Strikeouts; No Way for the Yankees," *New York Times*, September 11, 1999.

34 Ibid.

35 Gordon Edes, "The Only King of the Hill; Martinez Whiffs 17 in One-Hit Masterpiece," *Boston Globe*, September 11, 1999.

36 Ibid.

37 Krasner, *Pedro Martinez*, 11.

38 Mike Dodd, "Indians Rally for 3-2 Victory; Red Sox's P. Martinez Injures Back," *USA Today*, October 7, 1999.

39 Mark Blaudschun, "Solid Mound for Martinez; Ramon Makes Strong Pitch for Sox," *Boston Globe*, October 10, 1999.

40 Michael Madden, "Martinez Improving; Injured Ace Willing to Pitch In," *Boston Globe*, October 11, 1999.

41 Jay Greenburg, "Pedro Pulls a Paul Revere: Rides to Red Sox Rescue in Clincher," *New York Post*; also: Krasner, *Pedro Martinez*, 15; also: Sean McAdam, "The Playoffs—What a Big Relief to Have Pedro Back," *Providence Journal*.

42 Schaefer, 6.

43 Greenburg, "Pedro Pulls a Paul Revere," *New York Post*; also: Krasner, *Pedro Martinez*, 9; also: McAdam, "The Playoffs," *Providence Journal*.

44 Justice, "Red Sox, Martinez Punch Out Indians; Ace No-Hits Tribe Over 6 Relief Innings," *Washington Post*, October 12, 1999.

45 Krasner, *Pedro Martinez*, 15; also: McAdam, "The Playoffs," *Providence Journal*.

46 Jack Curry, "Martinez Does the Job with Ease," *New York Times*, October 17, 1999.

47 Glenn Stout and Richard A. Johnson, *Red Sox Century* (Boston, Mass.: Houghton-Mifflin, 2004), 442.

48 Edes, "KO For Martinez; Duel Turns into Mismatch of Century as Sox Shred Clemens," *Boston Globe*, October 17, 1999.

Chapter 5

49 Krasner, *Pedro Martinez*, 53.

50 Brian Lewis, "Pedro Pumped Up for Bronx Battle," *New York Times*, May 28, 2000.

51 Michael Gee, "Unparalleled Pedro—Martinez Acts as One-Man Dam," *Boston Herald*, July 24, 2000; also: Jeff Horrigan,

"Baseball; Pedro's Gem Shines,"
Boston Herald, July 24, 2000.

52 Gee, "Unparalleled Pedro,"
Boston Herald, July 24, 2000.

53 Chris DeLuca, "Sox Throw in
Towel as Martinez Fans 15,"
Chicago Sun-Times, July 24,
2000.

54 Bob Hohler, "Pedro Throws a
Masterpiece," *Boston Globe*,
July 24, 2000.

55 Burt Graeff, "Martinez Defends
Throwing at Diaz; Boston
Pitcher Surprised by Tribe's
Response," *Cleveland Plain
Dealer*, May 1, 2000.

56 Phil O'Neill, "Sox Get Minor
Scrapes in Major Scrape,"
Worcester Telegram & Gazette,
August 30, 2000.

57 Tony Massarotti, "Baseball;
Pedro Calm, Courageous,"
Boston Herald, August 30, 2000.

58 Krasner, *Pedro Martinez*, 51.

59 Hohler, "Martinez Getting
Antsy; Red Sox Ace Sees
Promising Signs," *Boston Globe*,
August 11, 2001.

60 Gordon Edes, "A Curse? A Spell?
Ghosts?" in Baseball Writers of
the *New York Times* and the
Boston Globe, The Rivals: The
Boston Red Sox vs. the New York
Yankees: An Inside History
(New York: St. Martin's Press,
2004), 162.

61 Krasner, "Red Sox Journal—
Good Start for Martinez Leaves
Everybody Happy," *Providence
Journal*, February 27, 2002.

62 Edes, "A Curse? A Spell?
Ghosts?" in *Baseball Writers*, 153.

63 Ibid., 163.

Chapter 6

64 Sean McAdam, "Bullpen Wastes
Another Strong Start by

Martinez," *Providence Journal*,
April 6, 2003.

65 Tyler Kepner, "Babe, Bucky,
Buckner, Boone," in *Baseball
Writers*, 182.

66 Sam Borden, "Controversy over
Martinez Pitches Evokes Strong
Reactions," Knight Ridder
Tribune News Service, July 7,
2003.

67 "Yanks Brush Off the Bosox;
Boss Unhappy with Pedro's
Inside Pitching," *Toronto Star*,
July 6, 2003.

68 Anthony McCarron, "Yankees,
Mussina Stop Sox, Martinez,"
Knight Ridder Tribune News
Service, July 7, 2003.

69 "Yanks Brush Off the Bosox,"
Toronto Star, July 6, 2003.

70 Shaughnessy, "Sox Lose Game 3
Melee: Yanks Frustrate Boston in
Wild Playoff, 4-3," *Boston Globe*,
October 12, 2003.

71 Bob Hohler, "Star-Crossed
Afternoon; Martinez and
Ramirez Were in Middle of It
All," *Boston Globe*, October 12,
2003.

72 Ibid.

73 Ibid.

74 Ronald Blum, "Take That,
Bambino: The Red Sox Rally
Past the Yankees to Force a
Deciding Game 7," *San Antonio
Express-News*, October 16, 2003.

75 Ibid.

76 Kepner, "Babe, Bucky, Buckner,
Boone," in *Baseball Writers*, 185.

77 Dave Sheinin, "Boone Bids
Boston Adieu; 11th Inning HR
Caps Comeback, Sends Yankees
to World Series," *Washington
Post*, October 17, 2003.

78 John Harper, "Boone Ends His
Swoon," *New York Daily News*,
October 17, 2003.

79 Sheinin, "Boone Bids Boston Adieu," *Washington Post*, October 17, 2003.

80 Mark Hale, "Pedro: Blame Me," *New York Post*, October 17, 2003.

81 Baseball Writers, 169; also, Sheinin, "Boone Bids Boston Adieu," *Washington Post*, October 17, 2003.

Chapter 7

82 Hohler, "Shaky Start Bad Inning Does in Martinez as Sox Lose Season Opener," *Boston Globe*, April 5, 2004.

83 Ibid.

84 Massarotti, "Pedro Gets It Right; His Changing Style Remains Dominant," *Boston Herald*, April 26, 2004.

85 Bob Klapisch, "Sox in Stunned Disbelief after 'Unbelievable' Loss," *Bergen Record*, July 1, 2004.

86 Ibid.

87 Ron Indrisane, "Martinez Made Sure Opponents Drew a Black," *Boston Globe*, September 4, 2004.

88 McAdam, "Sox Stopped in their Tracks—Martinez Late Lead Turns into Defeat," *Providence Journal*, September 25, 2004; also: Bill Ballou, "Frustrated Martinez Sounds off About Foes," *Worcester Telegram & Gazette*, September 25, 2004.

89 ———, "Sox Stopped in their Tracks—Martinez Late Lead Turns into Defeat," *Providence Journal*, September 25, 2004.

90 Horrigan, "Baseball; AL Division Series; Martinez, Sox Prove Two Good for Angels; Romp 8-3, Eye Sweep at Fenway," *Boston Herald*, October 7, 2004.

91 Tara Sullivan, "Pedro Comes to Daddy; but Red Sox Believe They'll See Pitcher at His Best," *Bergen Record*, October 13, 2004.

92 Jackie MacMullan, "Don't Pin This Loss on Him," *Boston Globe*, October 14, 2004; also: Mike DiGiovanna, "A Buzz-Cut for Boston," *Cincinnati Post*, October 14, 2004.

93 Stewart O'Nan and Stephen King, *Faithful: Two Diehard Boston Red Sox Fans Chronicle the Historic 2004 Season* (New York: Scribner, 2004), 363.

94 Edes, "He Gave Command Performance," *Boston Globe*, October 27, 2004.

95 Michael Silverman, "Baseball; World Champions; Pedro Soaks Up Title; Calls Win Highlight of his Career," *Boston Herald*, October 28, 2004.

Chapter 8

96 Steve Popper, "The Newest Hope; Pedro, GM Welcome Challenge that Awaits," *Bergen Record*, December 17, 2004.

97 Ibid.

98 Chuck Johnson, "Martinez Gets Respect He Wanted with Mets," *USA Today*, December 17, 2004.

99 Popper, "The Newest Hope," *Bergen Record*, December 17, 2004; also: Mark Hale, "An Amazin' Day for Pedro, Mets; New Face of Franchise All Smiles," *New York Post*, December 17, 2004.

100 Roger Rubin, "Pedro's Playhouse: Mets' Clubhouse Becomes the Place to Be," *New York Daily News*, December 26, 2004.

101 Ibid.

102 Bob Condotta, "At Last Mariners Get Better of Pedro; Seattle 4

New York Mets 1; Team Snaps 0-13 Skid Against Mets Ace," *Seattle Times*, June 19, 2005.

103 Marty Noble, "Martinez Baffles Marlins in Miami,"

www.mlb.com, May 28, 2005.

104 Ibid.

105 Ben Couch, "Pedro Dazzles Home Crowd," *www.mlb.com*, June 8, 2005.

Bibliography

Books

Baseball Writers of the *New York Times* and the *Boston Globe*. *The Rivals: The Boston Red Sox vs. the New York Yankees: An Inside History*. New York: St. Martin's Press, 2004.

Gallagher, Jim. *Latinos in Baseball: Ramon Martinez*. Childs, Md.: Mitchell Lane Publishers, 2000.

———. *Latinos in Baseball: Pedro Martinez*. Childs, Md.: Mitchell Lane Publishers, 1999.

Krasner, Stephen. *Pedro Martinez*. Philadelphia, Pa.: Chelsea House Publishers, 2002.

Montville, Leigh. *Why Not Us? The 86-Year Journey of the Boston Red Sox Fans from Unparalleled Suffering to the Promised Land of the 2004 World Series*. New York: PublicAffairs, 2004.

O'Nan, Stewart, and Stephen King. *Faithful: Two Diehard Boston Red Sox Fans Chronicle the Historic 2004 Season*. New York: Scribner, 2004.

Schaefer, A.R. *Sports Heroes: Pedro Martinez*. Mankato, Minn.: Capstone High-Interest Books, 2003.

Shaughnessy, Dan, and Stan Grossfield. *Fenway: A Biography in Words and Pictures*. Boston, Mass.: Houghton Mifflin, 1999.

Stewart, Mark. *Pedro Martinez, Pitcher Perfect*. New York: Children's Press, 2000.

Stout, Glenn, and Richard A. Johnson. *Red Sox Century*. New York: Houghton Mifflin, 2004.

Periodicals

Shaughnessy, Dan. "The Man at Ease: A Conversation with Pedro Martinez." *Boston Globe*, October 3, 1999, A1.

Smith, Chris. "Los Mets." *New York Magazine*, March 7, 2005, 22ff.

Web sites

Baseball Reference
www.baseball-reference.com

Online Encyclopedia: Pedro Martinez
http://en.wikipedia.org/wiki/Pedro_Martinez

Pedro Martinez Bio
http://www.jockbio.com/Bios/Pedro/Pedro_bio.html

New York Mets Official Site
www.mets.com

Haven for the Diehard Red Sox Fan
www.redsoxdiehard.com

Pedro Martinez Profile
http://sports.espn.go.com/mlb/players/profile?statsId=4875

Pedro Martinez Statistics
http://sportsillustrated.cnn.com/baseball/mlb/players/4875/

Further Reading

Books

Boston Globe. *Believe It: World Series Champion Boston Red Sox & Their Remarkable 2004 Season*. Chicago, Ill.: Triumph Books, 2004.

Gallagher, Jim. *Latinos in Baseball: Pedro Martinez*. Childs, Md.: Mitchell Lane Publishers, 1999.

Krasner, Stephen. *Pedro Martinez*. Philadelphia, Pa.: Chelsea House Publishers, 2002.

O'Nan, Stewart, and Stephen King. *Faithful: Two Diehard Boston Red Sox Fans Chronicle the Historic 2004 Season*. New York: Scribner, 2004.

Schaefer, A.R. *Sports Heroes: Pedro Martinez*. Mankato, Minn.: Capstone High-Interest Books, 2003.

Shalin, Mike. *Pedro Martinez: Throwing Strikes*. Champaign, Ill.: Sports Publishing, 1999.

Stewart, Mark. *Pedro Martinez, Pitcher Perfect*. New York: Children's Press, 2000.

Index

Picture Credits

About the Author

Tom Lashnits is a writer and editor specializing in history, culture, biography, and the economy. Early in his career, he worked as a researcher and writer at Time Inc., where among his many assignments he reported on Hank Aaron's record-breaking home run career. For a number of years, he was an editor at *Reader's Digest* magazine. He developed feature articles, edited issues of the magazine, and managed several departments. Lashnits is author of *The Columbia River* in the Chelsea House series RIVERS IN AMERICAN LIFE AND TIMES and *Recep Tayyip Erdogan* in the series MAJOR WORLD LEADERS.